I0479853

Unleashing
GROWTH

15 GROWTH MARKETING HACKS
EVERY ENTREPRENEUR SHOULD KNOW

RAGHAVENDRA HUNASGI

Raghav is a true Growth Marketing Zen Master — Daily Herald

notionpress
.com

INDIA · SINGAPORE · MALAYSIA

Notion Press

No.8, 3rd Cross Street
CIT Colony, Mylapore
Chennai, Tamil Nadu – 600004

First Published by Notion Press 2020
Copyright © Raghavendra Hunasgi 2020
All Rights Reserved.

ISBN 978-1-64899-697-9

Everything I do in my life including countless hours of writing, re-writing, and editing of this book would not have been possible without the unconditional support of, Shruti.

To Shruti, and my two greatest blessings and joy of my life.

– Yukta and Yagna.

Testimonials

"Raghav is a true Growth Marketing Zen Master"

"If Raghav is involved and he is part of your boardroom then know you are up to something big – he is a badass CMO."

– Anil Mishra, Podcaster (Pathfinder : Growth Stories for Personal Success)

The San Diego Union-Tribune

"Raghav is Father of Growth Marketing."

"Raghav is a game changing Growth Marketer – he has perfected the art of 10X mindset in everything he does."

– ASIA CMO Council

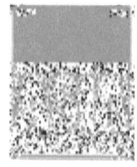

"New age corporate Growth Marketing Guru. If you have Raghav on your team – you have just added 100X horsepower to your marketing engine. Raghav is equal to growth and he is transformation Guru."

– ASIA Inc 500.

"A master of his craft and catalyst of Growth – Raghav is a delight to work with."

Extremely practical, insightful, and full of tips and tricks, *Unleash Growth* should be read not just by aspiring entrepreneurs but anyone seeking growth in business. Raghav himself is an example of how to grow your business 100X – a bestselling author, highly sought–after speaker, successful entrepreneur, high– profile CMO, and growth marketing Zen Master. I recommend anyone seeking growth read this, better read it twice or maybe thrice. This will be your growth blueprint.

– Rama Iyer, CIO of t– Hub (world's largest start– up ecosystem)

If you have to read only one book in marketing this is it. Buy it, read it, implement it, and see your business grow.

– Mark Fritz, Author, Leadership Coach, and Entrepreneur

Raghav has brought unparalleled growth to many start– ups and public listed companies in the past 10 years, and this book shows you how. A must– read if you are aspiring to grow.

– Avelo Roy, Managing Director of Kolkata Ventures

Raghav Hunasgi's book, 15 Growth Marketing Commandments, is practical, relevant and addresses the pain points faced by entrepreneurs trying to scale. It is based on Raghav's own experience, not on just theoretical knowledge, and is therefore so much richer and more useful. I love the "plug and play" and "mix and match" approach. Because that is the only way enterprises are going to survive and prosper in the post– Covid world. No single marketing strategy is going to cut it anymore. It works for enterprises as well, by the way, not just start– ups.

– Malavika R Harita, Founder & CEO at Brand Circle, Board of Governors, IIM Vishakapatnam and Advisory board member of the NSRCEL of IIM Bangalore.

Contents

Preface

The Birth of Growth Marketing Commandments

It all started in Naperville, Chicago in May 2018. After successfully running the North America Marketing for a large public listed company for five years, it was time to hit refresh. It was time to learn, unlearn, and relearn the new tactics of marketing. The quest was to invent the framework of Growth Marketing and design a process/method that would help anyone to ace consistently and be at the top of the game.

According to Singular's report on The State of the CGO, over 14% of companies in the US have a Chief Growth Officer, 29% of the organizations have the head of growth and 41% of the companies have growth marketers. It was about time to re-define the role of a marketer. That is exactly what I set out to do at Evolutyz Corp.

When I took over the role of Chief Marketing Officer my constant fervor was to find those 10 or 15 ways that will fuel the growth of any organization. Fast forward twenty-four months - Evolutyz Corp is one of the fastest-growing IT products, platforms, and services companies and also North America's best places to work according to Inc. magazines 2020 ranking.

When I look back - I feel we have done something right. This book is the result of all the experiments that worked and helped us grow an organization 10X in the past two years. The 15 activities that took us to the next level are the commandments of growth marketing.

I wish you all the best in your growth marketing journey and hope this book will be a guiding force in taking your organization to the next level of the game.

– Raghavendra Hunasgi
Your Growth Marketing Zen Master

Acknowledgments

If you have heard my Ted talk you would know my life is a story of blessings and grace. This book is no different and could not have seen the light without the blessings of almighty God and my Guru "Sri Raghavendra Swamy".

I'm indebted to countless people who have touched my life in infinite ways and shaped me to be a good marketer. Each one of us has two options in everything we do – maintain the status quo and perish over a while, or define the new normal and create an everlasting impact. This book is to thank many lion heart entrepreneurs, thought leaders, and change-makers who chose the latter.

I sincerely thank:

Praneshachar & Shilaja, for always being there for me all the time.

My best friends – Rama Iyer, Srinivas Arasada, and Kiran T Jayanna.

Mohit Chitkara, T G Vishwa Prasad, Balaji Sampath, Sairam Vedam, Dr. Surabhi Rairam, Hanna Natt-falkang, Vineeth Vankara, Ram Kiran Dhulipala, Malvika Harita,

Srinivas Kollipara, Anil Mishra, Srinivasan & Parimala – for the unconditional friendship and support.

And the list goes on.

Last but not the least, I would like to thank my chief critic Swetha Muthukrishnan and her team for their tireless efforts in making this book so beautiful and joyful to read. They have been firm in making sure we deliver 100% quality to our readers.

Introduction

Today, marketing is not just a choice but a necessity. However, most companies are not in a position to go the long-drawn route of undertaking market research, starting with a slow and steady approach to build up their marketing and sales base.

Most start-up companies need growth marketing but cannot afford the time, the money, and the efforts that are required to build up their marketing base. But the only way they can avoid failure is by marketing the products or services they are offering.

Then what can you do in this situation?

We have put together some marketing growth hacks that will soon become your commandments based on which you can build up your go-to-market fast. Even if some of the commandments don't work for you, you have the option to fail fast and learn fast.

When you read through the commandments that we prescribe, do not be shocked if you get those flashes of "why didn't think of this myself?" moments. That is because our hacks are easy, based on commonsense, and very practical.

Starting with the way you approach social media, segmentation, positioning, shameless campaigning, or your brand personality, there is something for everyone.

And the best part? When you read this book, you will realize that others have already tread this path to find their success, so you have if not time-tested formulas, at least successful hacks.

Each of the commandments can be used on its own, or you can combine the ones that you feel will work best for your particular business. The examples are there to do just that; guide you on which commandment would work for which kind of business.

Some of them are a bit radical and may not be for the faint-hearted, but then, neither is marketing. Marketing takes a lot of courage, hard work, determination, and focus.

This book can provide you the base and the starting point for your marketing journey.

Be Bold, Loud, Personal, and Vulnerable

"Today, the world longs to hear not about your achievements but your struggles. There is nothing that brings you closer than shared pain."

In today's world, the flow of information is almost relentless, which in turn means that you need to catch people's attention; you should be unafraid to be bold and loud. But then, being loud and bold will only get you so far because everyone in the market is the same.

What you need for your brand to stand out is to become personal. People are curious about what makes a brand tick. They want to know about the struggles that they have gone through.

Let us take a moment to look at what marketing means. It means being able to make a connection with your audience. Once you have this link going with your desired audience, it becomes more comfortable to touch upon their needs and wants to position your product.

"

Be bold, loud, personal, and vulnerable

While this may sound counter-intuitive, it is not. There is noise in the market, and if you want to be heard, you need to be loud and bold. However, that is not all... you need to stand out and touch your audience's hearts for that to happen, you need to be personal and let them see your vulnerability.

However, the first connection is not at all easy to make and maintain. You need a mix of all the qualities mentioned above, to be able to make inroads into the heart of the audience.

Let us take each part separately and then put them together.

Why do you need to be loud?

This question is easy enough to answer with the way the market is right now. There are so many brands, each shouting out their story for people to hear.

It is logical to assume that if you want your customers to listen to your voice in a crowded marketplace, you need to be loud. But is that enough?

We all know that people do not really like loud people because they come across as domineering and show-offish. This is where the personal aspect comes in.

We, as people, like to relate to others as people, not as companies or brands. We want to know that others are like us, with flaws, struggles, and having committed mistakes.

That is why we all love the story of the founder of KFC. Colonel Sanders did not even achieve fame until he reached 62 and became wealthy at 75. His background, his work ethics, his struggles, his many misses before his ultimate success are some of the aspects of his story that makes us feel warm and hopeful inside.

At the bottom of their hearts, most humans want validation that what they are facing and their failures are not faults but the foundation of a successful future.

How can you be loud yet personal? The answer lies in showing your vulnerability. When it comes to translating your loud, personal, and vulnerable tone of voice to the digital way of marketing, it is a delicate balance.

Here are some tips on how to do it: Relate to pain points

The main mistake that most brands make when it comes to positioning themselves on digital media is talking about what is great about their product or service.

You may ask, 'isn't that the point of marketing?'. Well, not really. What we want to tell people is that we know what is troubling them and that we understand their pain. Once you talk to people about their pain points, not only are their brains more receptive, they will also be more likely to loosen their purse strings.

For instance, instead of going on about how great their GPS and mobile network for their drivers is, a taxi or cab service needs to focus on the pain of being stranded without transport.

How vulnerable being without the means of transportation can be for a woman leaving the office late at night can be. Or how anxious a person can get when they have to catch a flight but cannot find transportation and so on.

This is an example of a product that is being sold from a business to customer (B2C). However, marketing can become a tad complicated when it is a business to another business (B2B).

You need to showcase your company products in a way that shows empathy, deep understanding of your customers' pain points, but without coming across as too sentimental.

In the business world, companies will make purchase decisions based on the understanding that the selling company has for their sector and their technical expertise in solving these problems.

Does this mean that the loud, personal, and vulnerable formula does not apply here?

No, it still applies, but it has to be dressed differently. While the product you are selling is to another business, at the end of the day, you are still dealing with humans.

An excellent example that you can see of marketing to other businesses done with this formula is that of accounting software. It showcases people who are heading essential roles in their respective companies, losing their peace of mind because their finance functions are not in order.

The accounting software then goes on to demonstrate how it solves their problems and helps them keep their peace of mind.

Show them the steps

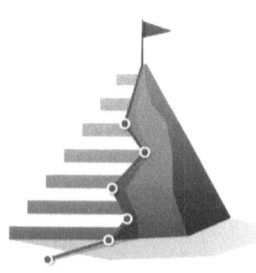

When you studied in school, you were often told that not only should you give the right answer to the math problem you are solving, but also show the work you did to arrive at the solution. In fact, many teachers will even tell you that you will get part of the marks if you show the work and your answer is wrong.

Well, apply that philosophy to your digital marketing efforts. When you think about it, it becomes apparent why you should do this. We, as humans, value anything that is hard to come by. Anything that is instant and easy may not have that much value though we will still use it.

And when it comes to digital marketing and sales, we know that we often do not touch base with the customer till the very end when we are closing the deal. How will the customer know how much thought, research, and efforts have gone into the product or service they are buying.

It takes a lot of courage, but showcasing the often not-so-attractive efforts that go into delivering a product or service needs to be shown to customers. Once again, it comes to not just putting in efforts, but showing it too.

It can be as simple as recording a video of your production process or showcasing how many misses you have had before you came up with the final product or service can do that trick.

Be absolutely realistic

While this is a cliché, it is also true; the truth will out. This is why you must confess to any misses or mistakes from your end before it gets exposed in some other way. And believe us, when we say it will be detected and at that time, you will look as if you were covering up, which is never a good thing.

An example that comes to mind is that of online shopping where products are wrongly delivered, sometimes not as per product description or any other missteps. These mistakes and misses could occur due to any number of reasons.

Human errors, intention to cheat, mistaken or missed steps, but you will find that people are more inclined to go back to the same site if the truth is not hidden or brushed off.

It is the same when you take B2B. However, the turnaround may take longer here because the investment is higher, and more people are involved in decision making.

Make no apologies

Once again, this may seem like a contradiction of what we have said earlier. However, when you examine it a little more in-depth, you realize that it is not.

Your product or service, no matter how big or small or how flawed or perfect it is, is yours, and that is what you can offer to your customers. It is possible that your competition has a better product or provides the same product or service at a lesser price.

The thing about today's world of information access and excess is that customers are likely to know everything. By everything, we mean literally everything—the price, the features, the flaws, the advantages, the differentiators, etc.

They probably know more details about the options in the market than you and your marketing team put together. That is why our advice to marketers around the globe is not to be apologetic about any aspect of their product or service.

The idea here is not to come across as having an attitude of 'take it or leave it' but rather that of saying 'we know the value that our product or service can bring to you, which is why we believe our pricing is fair.'

It is good to let the customer know that like them, you are in this for the profit and that you will build this in the pricing. Often, customers have this habit of digging deep into the costing details and expecting to be given something at that price.

However, the business does not work that way, and you need to make this clear in the way you position your product. To borrow a very popular phrase, 'because your product or service is worth it.'

Test your knowledge with this simple test

1. Why do you need to be loud as a marketer in today's world? Because:

   a. People like loud noises
   b. The market is crowded
   c. Making loud noises is in fashion
   d. Loud equals successful

2. Why does being truthful and vulnerable matter? Because:

   a. The truth will always come out, and then you will be vulnerable
   b. There is no way to hide the truth forever, and people relate to vulnerability
   c. The true path is the way forward for those who don't want to be seen as vulnerable
   d. Truth can make you look sincere and being vulnerable adds a human element

3. How do you balance your loud brand personality to make it more likable?

   a. Offer freebies every step of the way
   b. Throw in some entertainment to keep them coming
   c. Add a personal touch to make your brand approachable
   d. Keep shouting till you are heard and accepted

02 If You Must Copy, Do it From the Best but Do it with a Twist

"If you believe that there is no such thing as originality, you are not wrong. But copying is a science and art; you need to do it with finesse!"

Is everything we see around us original? Not really! Because we as a race are running out of original ideas. We are not saying that there are no original ideas out there, but just that, not everyone can wait around for inspiration to strike and to go to market with an original product or service.

Leave alone an original product or service, in today's fast-paced world; it may become challenging to wait for an original marketing campaign. But not to despair; all you need to do is become smart and do some research to come up with a plan that you can emulate.

"

If you must copy, do it from the best but do it with a twist

When you start new in the marketing world, there may be no time to do your research and look at use cases. The best hack at this stage is to copy from the best. There is nothing wrong with it as long as you manage to personalize it with a unique twist to make it stand out.

After all, there are many great ideas out there, and most of these have gone through the grind, subjected to a lot of due diligence, and put a lot of thought into it. But the thing about copying someone is that you need to do it smartly.

How do you copy smartly and own the idea that you have picked someone else?

Let us start by telling you that even copying someone else's marketing strategy, inspiration, plan, and making it your own can be hard work. In fact, we insist that you spend a lot of time, thoughts, and efforts in selecting the right one and then adding a twist that makes it your own.

Step 1: Map what you want to achieve

Any plan that you are working on will never work unless you have mapped the starting point and the place where you want to end up. For instance, you are in the business of selling software, and you want to be seen as the next Infosys.

It would help if you knew your offering in and out. That is, not only the benefits but also the flaws. If anything, knowing what your product or service cannot do is just as crucial (if not more) than what it can do.

Here is where good old-fashioned marketing fundamentals will come into play. That is, the price, product, promotion, and positioning will come into place.

Dive deep into how you see the product (which buyer persona does it fit?) who is going to benefit from it, does it have only utilitarian value or does it have prestige value?

Do you think pricing can be aspirational, or does it have to be very low pricing because it does not have any prestige attached? What do you think the break-up, the discounts, bulk pricing, etc., be like?

Do you see any new uses that your product team has not factored in? For example, accounts payable software also helps with the procurement function, contract management, compliance, audits, etc. A company may invest in the product for these benefits and not just the AP automation aspect.

Create a persona for the typical customer that would be buying your product. Analyze who will be:

- Attracted to the product
- Convincing the decision-maker about the purchase
- The final decision maker

Step 2: Look at what your competitors are doing

In this step, you should stick to only your product, sector, and direct competition. However, that is only the starting point. Examine what they have done and how they have done it.

More importantly, learn how effective it has been because this aspect should give you an idea of how much you need to spend to bring about effective results.

The reason you need to study your direct competition is not necessarily to copy what they are doing directly but rather avoid coming across as a duplicate of your competition. You definitely want to avoid that because then you will just become a has-been me-too in this aggressive and overcrowded market.

However, these are the points that you need to look at:

- How they have positioned their persona pain points
- What is their pricing like; do they have discounts?
- Their unique selling proposition (most economical, most advanced, does some function better, certified by some known agencies, etc.)
- What is the talk surrounding their product on social media?
- How good are they in after-sales service?

Keep all these factors in your product thinktank so that you can take what works best for you and avoid their pitfalls.

Doing a competition analysis is not only crucial to get your product or service right and in a competitive position but also as preparation for customer queries and questions.

In many instances, it may make sense to emulate what your competition has done directly, but with your own differentiator. A sterling example of this is the Flipkart versus Amazon story. The promoters of Flipkart are actually ex-employees of Amazon who walked off with knowledge of the internal workings to start a similar company.

Their differentiator? The desi advantage! But this formula may not always work. One of the best ways to repurpose an idea is by seeking inspiration from unrelated sectors. That way, you have the advantage of being unique and successful.

Step 3: Go beyond your niche and look at other sectors

What we are talking about here may be confusing unless we start with an example. Take, for instance, luxury brands like Rolex and Mercedes. At first glance, there is nothing in common between them; one of them is a watch, and the other is a vehicle.

However, when you dive deeper, you realize that they do share something in common. They are both luxury brands. Owning a Rolex or a Mercedes goes beyond the purpose they serve—which is that of keeping time or transportation.

Owning a Rolex or driving a Mercedes immediately sets you apart. It shows the onlooker that you not only have the affordability but also has a certain amount of class.

The idea behind this example was to show you that while you are looking for inspiration beyond your niche is to seek a common thread. For instance, the product you are selling is sustainable energy like a solar cooker, which uses sunlight to cook food and help you save money on cooking fuel and help the environment.

In this example, you can look at companies that are selling organic products like food, drinks, etc. While both the products are different, they share a commonality in the sense that both of them focusing on conserving the environment. One of them focuses on saving fossil fuel while the other wants to reduce the use of chemicals in the production of food and drink.

Both these niches would focus on the green-inclined and environmentally minded people, and the marketing would focus on the consumers who are the decision-makers in their respective domains, whether it is the home or the office.

Doing this will give you the right direction and ensure that you do not come across like a me-too product. On the other hand, you will be able to save a lot on time and effort for the creation of your marketing strategy.

Make sure that the niche that you end up emulating has a common thread running along with your sector or is relatable in some way.

Step 4: Collect all the aspects you like

Even as we speak about two different approaches to the same end, we are not saying that you have to go with one or the other. What we mean is that it is all about learning what others are doing, how they are doing it, and the kind of results they are getting with it.

But once you do, you need not pick one path to follow. For instance, you may like the pricing strategy of your direct competitor, but like the promotional aspect of the product in your niche. Who is to say that it has to be one or the other.

This is where making it your own with a personal twist comes in. Start by writing down what each of the product strategies (the direct competitor and the same-niche product) are doing. What is the messaging they are putting across?

Are they talking about the pricing advantage? Or are they making pricing secondary and only focusing on the green advantage? Is their focus on one of the trending topics that have become the buzzwords in social media today?

Or are they altogether talking about being ahead of the curve? Once again, it would be prudent for you to go back to the basics of marketing, which is the product, positioning, promotion, and pricing.

Do you think that the product and positioning of the product in your niche are spot on, but their promotional strategy will not work with your vision? Do you feel that the pricing could be tweaked based on the cost aspects and the prestige value that your product brings to the customer?

The advantage of trying to emulate more than one marketing strategy is that you get to pick and choose what works for you and discard what does not.

While the approach we are talking about is simple, it is by no means easy. You will need to be diligent in your research and delve deeper into the nuances of their thinking behind the way your competitor and niche company is pricing, positioning, and promoting their product.

Fortunately, there is a hack to do that today as most companies are online and, more importantly, on social media. You can glean a lot of insights into what their audience is talking about. We have deliberately used the word 'audience' here instead of customers because not everyone on the social media of different brands are their customers.

Today, you have a new breed of people who think it is their duty to have and offer an opinion. These people may not be paying to buy your product, but they can influence the buying decision.

One of the best ways to collect all the aspects that you like is to write it down on a thought board.

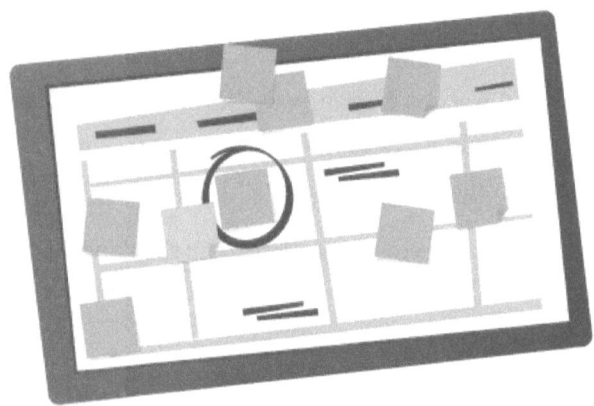

Creating a thought board may seem to be too tedious, but it can help you envision where your thought process is leading you and will also help showcase your strategy to others.

Step 5: Curate what would work and what would not

Not everything that you like about your competitors and your niche market would work for you. And in some instances, even if they would work, they may not be practical in the timeframe and budget (both resources and funds) you have.

In some cases, it would be a good idea to try a few aspects in the beginning and have a phased plan for the rest of the steps. At this point, it would be a good idea to add people with a more operational and practical bent of mind to your thinktank.

People who are used to carrying out plans and the team that manages the funds are likely to be a bit more pragmatic in their approach. They could help you figure out which of the aspects that you have picked out can work and which ones would not.

While in some instances, such people have been accused of throwing cold water on your dreams, such practical people are critical to the success of your marketing plan. These are the people who will keep you grounded and on-track.

But if you and your marketing team are passionate about a particular aspect, you can always push your case forward and get permission to try it out.

It would help if you had some numbers to back up your point, which again emphasizes the need to be thorough and well-prepared with your numbers. While many claim that marketing is a creative process, and it is, but it is also grounded in figures.

The numbers game starts right with the portion of the audience you want to target, the amount you want to spend on your efforts, the number of leads you want to generate, and the overall return on investment that your company can expect from your efforts.

Step 6: Do a dry run with a few people

One of the cautions that all marketers would do good to keep in mind is that it is always better to fail small at first before you move on to succeed in a big way. Marketing is an activity that will happen in the public eye, and with the whole world going digital, the world is like one big community.

That is why the top management often asks the marketing department to do a dry run. Doing a dry run is not just good sense but also a necessity because the lessons you will learn from this exercise can be invaluable.

One of the amusing examples that come to mind is of a very old case study where Brylcreem was marketed in Africa. In the beginning, it did exceptionally well, but later it was discovered that people did not really know what the product was about.

They used Brylcreem as a bread spread instead of using it to style their hair as it was supposed to be used. A dry run in the market, in this instance, would have helped the marketers to position their product better.

There are many ways in which you can do a dry run. For example, for a costly product, it can be with a few handpicked group of people who would be able to give you feedback. Or if it is a relatively new product but of lesser value, you can market it in a particular market, which is known to have the right mix of people.

Another approach would be to go is by putting together a test group that can provide you a response to the way you have positioned your product. Or you can add an exclusivity tag to your product by letting people buy it only by invitation – like One Plus brand.

When you are doing a dry run, try and get as diverse a mix as possible of people to give their feedback to you. What is more, there are two ways to approach this. One is by telling the group of people what you are doing and why you are doing it. The other option is by not providing complete information to the test group of people.

Some companies often do a dry run within their company's extended group, like the families and friend circle of employees to control costs. However, the element of honesty may be reduced because of the vested interests of the audience.

Step 7: Add your differentiator and run with it

You have done your research, you have applied your collective brains on it, run it by the money people, and done a dry run. Now is the moment of truth—how to add a differentiator and run with it?

If you want, you can add a standard differentiator that has always worked for your brand in the past. However, often, with new companies, there is no history to draw from. When this happens, it is time to be bold and create a differentiator.

Here are some of the easiest and most common differentiators that you can use:

- Your differentiator will, later on, become your brand identity and therefore needs some thought. But it need not be something too elaborate. It can be something as simple as a hashtag that you come up with and use in all your marketing campaigns. Ensure that it is politically correct and inoffensive so that you can use it generously

- Your differentiator can be something as simple as your color theme or a particular color palette to give you a broader choice in the future. For instance, your color theme could consist of certain shades that can be mixed, matched, or used individually

- A tagline is another differentiator that will stay in the minds of your audience. It is a good idea to have a couple of options in mind to try out during your dry run to ensure that it packs the punch that you want it to

- If your budget permits, it can be about one celebrity who becomes your brand ambassador, but this may not be a great option if you are just stepping into the market. Instead of go for something iconic like being the brand that supports change (Surf) or portrays women in leadership roles (L'Oreal)

- And if you are feeling really adventurous, you can go for negative posturing (remember the old Onida ads?). For instance, how people change into something else when they realize that you possess something or a product that drives you crazy (Center Fresh chewing gum)

Now that you have your marketing strategy in place, do not fail to plan, or else you will have to plan to fail. No marketer has ever said that he or she was spontaneous when it comes to executing his or her plan and had a resounding success.

If anything, have a plan A and back it up with plan B if there are any problems.

Test your knowledge with this simple test

4. What are the two segments of the market that you can copy from?

   a. Your competitor and the lowest-performing opponent in your segment

   b. Companies in your niche and the best marketer in the world

   c. Companies that are in direct competition with you and companies that are doing well in a similar niche

   d. Companies that have no relation with your segment but whose marketing strategy is shocking and disruptive

5. Which one of these represents competitors and companies for a similar niche?

   a. Etsy-Ebay and Pottery Barn-Ikea

   b. Suzlon-Whole Foods and Samsung-Apple

   c. Mercedes-Heinz and Amazon-Alibaba

   d. Procter & Gamble-Nirma and CocaCola-Pepsi

6. What steps should you follow to come up with the right marketing strategy?

   a. Observe, curate, discuss, test, add some value, and launch

   b. Copy, paste, plan, launch, and make changes when required

    c. Learn from others, copy correctly, and make sure to plan well

    d. View, convey, convince, test, launch without changes

Always Hope for the Best, But Plan for the Worst

"Success is not about being an optimist or a pessimist but about being a positive realist!"

What? What? Well, read it the title and the quote again to realize what we mean. Marketing is not for the faint-hearted and if you think that it is about luck, chance, and a lot of happy coincidences, then think again.

Planning well and in detail and then backing up your plan with another superb plan will be the way to go. But having said that, planning is never simple because not only do you plan with meticulous detail but also build in a failsafe in case things go wrong.

Preparing to succeed but with a parachute to save you from crashing is not a natural activity to carry out.

"

Always hope for the best, but plan for the worst

Marketers across the world are seen as optimistic and positive people, and that is how it should be. But you must be a realist too. Which is why all your plans should have back-up plans and many options.

How do you plan like this? Get the team right

A reliable marketing team can be worth its weight in gold. In the conventional sense, your marketing team should consist of an SEO team, content writers, graphic designers, the analytics team, social media experts, and a web and automation team, headed by a campaign manager.

We are not saying that your team should not have these people or rather these skills, they should, but you need to go a step beyond. You need to get different personalities together. What you need is the strategic thinker, along with the details person who will delve into every operational detail to get it right.

You also need a wildly imaginative person working alongside an absolute pessimist, and for good measure through in a realist in the mixture. By now, you must have realized what we are thinking about. We need them all—the fierce warrior, the constant worrier, the obsessive planner, the devil's advocate, the fantasy liver, and the numbers person—thrown in.

Ensure that you have a strong leader in place to manage this dream (or sometimes nightmare) team well. It will not be an easy task, but the results will be impressive.

Research continuously

While your dream team is fighting it out, make sure that you are researching continually. Talk to the sales and marketing teams of your competitor, scan the social media pages of your competition, learn to read between the lines of their content.

When you do this well, you will be able to glean where they are coming from and who their target is. If you have the budget for it, seek sources that can give you a peek into their plan and customers.

Make sure that your team is aware of what you are discovering from your continuous research. Ask them what they think. Run daily meetings where you post the findings of your study on the board with your conclusions. Spend no more than 3 minutes for each person to challenge or add to the conclusions on the board, along with their reasoning.

For better recall, you can even record the meetings to ensure that you do not miss out on any insight or input.

Go shopping with your competitor

Now, this is something that you should do as much as time, money, and people you can spare. It does not matter if you are copying from your competition—as suggested in the earlier chapter—or not because it is good sense to do so.

It is like you test the waters before you take the plunge. You want to learn what they are doing, why they are doing it, and, more importantly, what is right about what they are doing, and the aspects they are getting absolutely wrong.

You want to know why customers buy from them, what they feel when they buy from them and do they do it because they have to or because they want to.

This kind of research comes easy when your marketing is business-to-customer (B2C) rather than business-to-business(B2B). However, you can get around the shortcomings of not experiencing the entire purchasing experience in B2B by allowing yourself to be led more in-depth into the buyer's journey.

This will give you an idea about what they are offering to customers at every stage of the buying journey (awareness, consideration, decision). You will even be able to get a glimpse of their case studies, thought leadership, and other content pieces that they offer as part of their nurture flow.

Apart from ensuring that your whole team is well-versed with the Inbound Method of Marketing, shopping with competitors will help you hone your plan well.

Budget it right

Marketing budgets are perhaps the most discussed, argued, and fought over component in any business. The whole world (apart from the marketing team) believes that marketing budgets are a waste of money, while the marketing team struggles to juggle priorities and maximize the bang for their buck.

What should your budget look like?

If we are honest, we would say that your budget should look ambitious, but that is not always possible because most companies have a lot of conflicting demands on their resources, which are often limited.

Here are the main elements to include in your budget and the reasons why you should do it.

Let us face it; only organic marketing efforts are not going to pay off. You need a mix of paid marketing (ads on social media, PPC ads, hoardings, listings, PR, events, etc.) alongside your organic efforts (website, blogging, social media marketing, sharing on forums, etc.).

Your budget should then include each of these elements. There is no easy hack here to do this as the marketing budget needs detailed analysis and planning. Here is where having the naysayers, money counters, and pessimists in your team is going to pay off.

Budget big on paid efforts in the beginning

Purists in the digital marketing world believe that going for paid marketing is a shortcut, and this is true, but that does not mean you should not do it.

If anything, at the beginning of your marketing efforts, it is better to create a presence at once and continue to 'haunt' people. Have you ever looked at something out of curiosity, and then have it pop up at every site you visit? That happens with certain kinds of paid marketing efforts.

Do not stint on quality collateral

One piece of quality marketing collateral like an excellent video that touches the right chord in people can be effective, and you should go for it even if it is a bit expensive. Start your budgeting exercise with a list of collateral that you need to run your online campaigns.

You will realize that all marketing efforts will require money and efforts, whether it is organic or paid. The only difference is that most of the organic elements like design, content, webpage creation, and SEO will come from the team you have. But paid efforts will cost over and above these.

However, look at quality collateral and efforts in the beginning rather than a massive quantity of generic collateral. The start of your marketing campaign is when you need to make an impression in the mind of your audience and with the noise and competition that is there in the market already.

Be seen and heard consistently

Though people do not want to admit it, most of us are creatures of habit, and this is something that you have to capitalize on. In terms of the budgeting exercise, this translates to being prepared to spend money on campaigns to build up that rhythm, at least in the beginning.

Work on having your creatives in place well ahead of time to ensure that you can build up the rhythm in your marketing at the beginning itself.

Don't let go of your organic efforts

Organic efforts need money for the creation and not for distribution, which is why you need to budget for these, especially if your internal team cannot deal with all the creative work. Budget for paid and organic creatives with a special emphasis for more spending at the beginning of your efforts. As time goes on, and the analytics indicate that your brand has gained some momentum, you can ease on the paid efforts and continue with the organic efforts.

However, do make a provision for some money to be spent on paid campaigns for seasonal slumps and other eventualities.

Plan in detail about the budget timing of events

You will find that an event calendar—either from the internet or your own—is your best friend when it comes to budgeting. We are talking about events here because though most marketing takes place online, nothing can replace the importance of human contact and the kind of relationships that you can build at events.

Your budget should have not only some provisions for the attendance fees for events, the creation of collateral, and the giveaways at the event but also the travel and accommodation requirements of the team that will attend the event.

However, research and curate only those events that will work for your company and product and hone the budget according to the timing of these events. A simple way to do it is by doing a detailed need-want analysis. The idea is, needs trump wants when it comes to budgeting.

Ensure that you use your budget smartly

A budget is just an indicative list of expenses that you anticipate in the time to come; it is not a rule that if you have budgeted something, you have to spend it. Make sure that you need to spend the amount from your budget before you release the funds.

Take, for example, a meeting of CXOs that you are planning to participate in just before the festive season. The mileage you will get from this event is going to be astounding, and you need to have a presence there. Let us assume that you are planning to give away some branded merchandise at the event. Given the level of people who are participating, you have planned on an expensive giveaway.

However, when you rethink the giveaway, you realize that the event is just before festive season when the CXOs will anyway get a lot of gifts. What is more, the other companies in the event will also be planning giveaways.

It makes good sense to give something relatively cheap but memorable instead of splashing on an expensive giveaway, which may not have an impact.

Leave room for rework and relaunch

No plan will completely succeed at all times, and it is absolutely okay to accept that. In fact, go a step further and prepare for it. Ensure that you have a fallback budget that you can use to rework some aspects of your marketing campaign and relaunch it.

There is no shame in revisiting your campaign to look at what has gone wrong and make adjustments for the errors in it. If anything, it shows maturity and competence when you do this. However, do plan for this and make provisions in your budget for such rework.

After all, there are going to be no repercussions if you spend less than what you have budgeted for, but there will be a backlash if you spend more than what you have budgeted.

Keep monitoring

Plans fail all the time, and there is no shame in that; it is only when you do not monitor your plans and keep forging ahead despite evidence of failure, that you fail. Make monitoring a priority and nominate one person to do just that.

Ensure that the person-in-charge of monitoring has a passion for numbers and can look at patterns that keep occurring to do a root-cause analysis. Once you have the monitoring mechanism in place, you can look for what works and what does not to keep tweaking your plan.

Be open and matter of fact about what is going wrong, and instead of defending yourself and your team or blaming it on somebody or something, concentrate on the next steps.

Be ready with humble pie and leave your ego aside

In the world of marketing, where you and your team are responsible for delivering tangible results, there is no place for an ego trip. As we have mentioned in the earlier section, present negative results and the root causes to your management along with positive results.

Negative results can often be beneficial, providing you with valuable lessons for the time to come. For instance, running a campaign for corporate governance software on Facebook may not provide you with the best results. And if you have such a lesson that you have learned, it is good to document it and share it with the larger audience.

Make it a point to present the reasoning behind the move, the reasons that it did not work, and the steps you took to correct it. Doing this will ensure that you have presented the whole picture to the management and ensured that it does not reach them through other sources.

Keep your ears open for external factors

Marketing cannot happen in a vacuum; it has to take external and macro factors into consideration. Take, for instance, a pandemic like situation and imagine that you are marketing a travel package.

There simply is no point in spending big money on marketing your product in such a situation because there would be no takers due to the travel restrictions in our country and across the globe.

On the other hand, you could encourage people to share their past travel photos and memoirs to keep the momentum going till such time that the situation changes. While this will not get you any leads right now, it will keep your brand in people's minds.

Moreover, such efforts do not require much investment, and your team can carry this activity out organically. External factors can throw your plan off entirely or make it much better, which is why keeping an eye out or even subscribing to an industry newsletter is a good idea. Once again, a shortcut to do this is to subscribe to your competitor's newsletter.

Move on fast

Speed, not haste, is at the center of all marketing efforts and plans. You need to be quick in your reactions to changing situations, campaigns gone wrong, tweaks you need to make mid-campaign, or to stop specific spending.

To ensure that you can move on fast, be very clear on what you are looking for as an outcome from your marketing campaigns. In some cases, the objective may be to simply get more exposure to your brand, and in that case, your reaction can be accordingly.

But in most cases, marketing does not have the luxury of languishing in the background. In most cases, it is all about getting as many leads or sales as possible. In such instances, moving on fast from mistakes, and going on to making changes is essential.

But as we mentioned in the beginning, it cannot be about haste. Any change you make has to be well-considered but without sacrificing speed. It is a difficult ask, but then digital marketing is a challenging undertaking.

The idea behind any marketed-related plan is to ensure that you have mapped out all the outcomes, put in the details of the next steps, budgeted for the good and bad, and lastly, factored in external factors.

When you do this, you will have a plan that is realistic but positively oriented instead of a very conservative plan that will restrict your efforts or an overly optimistic one that may have negative repercussions.

Test your knowledge with this simple test

7. Why do you need to hope for the best but plan for the worst?

   a. Because it is more fun to do this and makes you look quirky
   b. Planning can be like jumping from a height, and you need to look down
   c. It is always better to have a back-up plan when things don't go as planned
   d. You need these justifications to explain things to your top management

8. What should the ideal marketing team consist of?

   a. The most creative and positive writers and designers you can get
   b. Simple but knowledgable technicians who will jazz up your website
   c. A mix of various skillsets and personalities to help maintain the balance
   d. People who are related to top management to help you get approvals

9. How to get started with the right customer experience?

   a. Educated guesses and simple insights from social media should work
   b. Research, test marketing, insights from competitors, and trials will help you

   c. Be guided with what your production folks have to say about your product or service

   d. Listen to what your finance and operation teams have to say and inculcate this

04 Start Social and Keep it Going Continuously

"In the world of marketing, there is no such thing as excess when it comes to social media success."

In today's world, as we move away further apart from each other physically, the need for human contact becomes even more intense. Before I jump into the marketing aspect, let us take a look at how the world has changed to bring context to the marketing hacks we are talking about.

When was the last time you came across a joint family with more than 2-3 generations living together? When was the last time you just walked into a neighbor or friend's house without prior notice? How much time has it been since you sent a birthday card (if you have ever done it at all) to a friend wishing them for their special day?

When was the last time—as a grown-up with a job—that you had an impromptu chat with your college or school friends in person? Or when was the last time your entire family sat down for more than one meal together at the table on a daily basis?

"

Start social and keep it going continuously

In the digital marketing world, there is no ignoring the social aspect. Go prominent and visible on social media, even if it means making up stuff and putting out content that you have 'borrowed' from elsewhere. Ask your whole team to do this.

As technology and communication evolves, ironically, we as humans have become distant from each other, at least in the physical sense. But all is not lost. We do need to connect, and that is why we often reach out to each other on social media, through telephone, or use other forms of technology to connect.

The need to connect, share, express, and comfort each other is always at the base of all human needs. There are always going to be exceptions who still like to do things 'old-school' and eschew social media. But those are not a very large portion of the population.

Now that we have taken a look at why social media has become such a vital cog in the machinery of our lives, it is time to look at how marketing can leverage this.

When it comes to buying experiences, customers today want brands to talk to them and not at them. Not surprisingly, this applies as much to business-to-business deals as to business-to-customer marketing. People want to know that you are listening to them. They want to know that you understand what they need and that you are prepared to help them meet the need or solve the problem.

Today, marketing is no longer just about telling how great your product is (though you have to do that too, but subtly) but about your in-depth knowledge of their business. Let us look at an example here:

Example 1:

Eating right, on-time, and without sacrificing taste is essential for an upcoming executive who juggles home, work, and social life. We have just the right solution for you!

Example 2:

Get the best, the tastiest, and the healthiest food at our shop! We are the most popular in your area, and we have been in this business for over two decades.

Both of the examples are aiming at the same audience. But the first one tells you that they understand what you need and would like to supply it to you. The main focus is on you. The content talks about how you need to manage so many things but still need tasty food that is healthy delivered on-time to you.

The second ad copy is all about how good the business is and how awesome they are. While this may work in some instances, the first example will remain in your brain because it touches your emotions.

Let us now start by looking at why you and your entire team needs to go social and keep going at it continuously.

Social media is the place to be for businesses today because it basically plays the role of those old-fashioned get-togethers we used to have. Whether it is the after office-grab-a-drink sessions to discuss the day or the gathering in front of our residences to exchange news of the day, all this happens on social media.

The young and restless like to be more visual and picture-oriented on sites like Instagram and Pinterest, while the slightly older ones like Facebook, and if you want to check out professional updates, then LinkedIn it is. And for those who like to keep it short and witty, it is Twitter.

People like to share, vent, comment, discuss and even silently watch on social media. How can a smart business miss this low-hanging fruit when it comes to its marketing efforts?

However, before you decide to jump into social media willy-nilly along with your marketing crew, wait and read on a little about the dos and don'ts.

It is not just about merely copying the post that your company puts on its handle and sharing it on one's social media space. There needs to be a structure and policy in place to ensure that your team's efforts pay off.

The rules of social media for your team needs to include the following:

Don't just copy content and share, but curate

As a marketing department, there could be a fair amount of content coming out of your division. Even as you encourage your team to share the posts on their own handles, you need to tell them it is okay not to share everything and they should curate what they want to share.

Often, when companies encourage their team to share company content on their personal accounts, people in their social cycle start unfollowing them because they are bored with a barrage of marketing content. The idea behind having your team sharing marketing content is for it to be consumed.

That is why you can have a social advocacy session where you can advise people on how to curate what works best for their group of social media contacts, and share accordingly.

Here is an example: One of your graphic designers has a lot of likeminded individuals in his or her contact list. When your marketing department has a video to share, then your graphic designer can share it along with his or her thoughts tagging some of his or her friends who are in the same profession.

Doing this will strike a chord that this group can relate to, and this will get the conversation going. When people join the conversation and talk about it, they may even share on their own pages leading to more engagement.

The idea is to have your team become an extended part of your digital marketing efforts but smartly and constructively.

Stay away from being rude and controversial

Being controversial is the new social media norm with people taking digs at each other and being openly rude. Even as a general rule, discourage your team from doing something like this when they share personal content.

However, you may not have that much control over what they share personally, but you can impose strict guidelines on how your company content is shared and how your employees react to comments on these posts. If possible, have your content and copywriters come up with witty and quirky comments for the queries and feedback people post on the shared content.

In some instances, it may pay off to be controversial and provocative on social media, and you could ask your team members to do this. But even as you do it, make sure that you have selected the right people to do it.

It is also an excellent practice to coach them in the right way to do this without coming across as obnoxious.

Do not just share, but invite people for discussions

When your team goes social, enable them to encourage people to talk with each other and the person posting it, instead of merely putting the post out there. How do you do this? It could be as simple as tweaking the content on the post.

For instance, instead of saying 'Going Green for all your energy needs can be a costly and long-drawn process,' you could say 'Let's discuss how we can ease your move from carbon fuels to green energy.' Or better still, ask a question. 'What problems are you facing while adopting green energy?'

Something as simple as this on a platform like LinkedIn will draw some feedback and comments. Even if the comments are from your competitor, make sure that you address them and offer them a chance to put forth their opinions. Ask your entire team (those who do not handle social media) to set aside an hour daily to engage with the comments and discussions on their posts.

Remember, people do not remember what you do for them, but how you made them feel? And interaction with people is an essential aspect of social media marketing.

Choose your channel wisely for maximum impact

All social media channels are not equal, and it is crucial to understand this from the beginning. Imagine you are selling water pumps to households, housing societies, and office buildings.

Here is a basic plan about what content you can have your team and company share on social media:

LinkedIn – Talk about the pain points of those who plan to buy water pumps for their requirements but are not sure what to look for. Offer a free resource to help them understand what is essential and what is not. Offer an ROI calculator, options for finance (if any), and a detailed sheet on what delays and disruptions they can expect during the process of installation.

Facebook, Twitter, and Instagram—Share a touching story of how having the right water pump helped one of your customers. This can include a selection of individual customers, housing societies, and office buildings. This needs to be warm and leave people with a fuzzy feeling when they read it. You can end it with a call to action that directs people on the next steps.

On Pinterest- Show them lovely pictures of how places have transformed because your water pumps have enabled them to beautify their surroundings. Something like a before and after should be the way to go because Pinterest is a lot about visuals.

Do not jump into conversations that are potentially damaging

Yes, social media is the place to see, be seen, join the conversation, discuss, offer your two cents, and generally keep the engagement going. However, some subjects will never become politically correct, and you and your marketing team need to avoid these like the plague.

Have strict guidelines to ensure that none of your team members find themselves amid such conversations. Make this a non-negotiable rule that you must inculcate as part of your onboarding process.

Take, for instance, Amazon, who, by their own admission, is one of the most customer-obsessed companies in the world. Not only do they put every employee who joins their company (on the customer service side) through a complete customer service associate training, taking calls, and solving problems, but also instruct them on how to conduct themselves on social media.

The concept is that each and every employee is considered a representative of the company, and the way they present themselves on social media is a reflection of the brand.

Have a whetting and approval process for press releases

Press releases are another aspect that you will need to regulate in terms of how you let your team share online. It has been seen that employees have the tendency to jump the gun and share a version of the press release on social media even before the company's official version is out.

When this happens, it may not always be to your advantage. Often, the result is a distorted version of the information reaching the market before it was supposed to be shared.

While it is challenging to prevent important updates from leaking out (the company grapevine works overtime), warn people that sharing on social media is strictly prohibited.

In fact, there should be a policy and process in place. It can start with the request for the creation of PR. Once this is done, it needs to go through some iterations and then approvals. Once the approved version is up on the website, send out an email to the marketing team that they may share it on the company's social media pages and their personal accounts if they want to.

Engage with stories on content creation where you were a part of it

Social media is all about the personal journeys, the raw bits, the reality bites, and the stories behind the scene. Many companies shy away from sharing this because they feel that they feel it makes them look unprofessional. However, the public loves the underdog and the human touch.

Make it a point to record the stories that you were a part of and share this on social media, complete with pictures that were clearly taken by non-professionals.

Why? The answer lies in our first hack about being loud, personal, and vulnerable. People are curious, but in a contrarian way, they are also easily bored.

People often want to know how and why something happened and who was involved in it. And if you are always going to present an even and bland façade to them, they may lose their interest and move on to the next exciting thing.

Test your knowledge with this simple test

10. Who in your team needs to be seen and heard on social media?

   a. Only the marketing leaders and the technical staff need to be on social media

   b. Social media is the sole responsibility of your social marketing team

   c. Most of your team if not the entire team, needs to be smartly present on social media

   d. It is confusing and counter-productive; that is why you should avoid social media

11. What are the rules to follow for your team participating in controversial topics on social media?

   a. Just jump in and give as good as you get. You can do what you please as long as people read your posts

   b. Be careful in the way you address controversies. If possible, seek the help of your content team to come up with quirky and witty answers that are not offensive

   c. Do whatever you please as long as you share all your company content on social media to get as much mileage as possible

   d. Keep it quiet and never share anything that relates to your company on your personal social media accounts

12. What should a company's policy on press releases?

    a. Share within the company internally and externally at the same time and then brief people to share on social media

    b. Make an internal announcement and then ask your entire team to share on social media to get the best exposure possible

    c. Put the press release on external media and then hope that your employees will look at it and share extensively on social media

    d. Never encourage people to share press releases on social media; it is supposed to be confidential even after you have posted it online

Being Helpful to Customers Always Helps—Even if it Means Talking up Competitors

"People seek kindness and information; why not be the source that serves them both?"

There is no dearth of information out there. It is all available to you and that too, in most instances, for free. But you have to make that effort to look for it. You have to think it through and then use the right words to search to get a horde of results, which you need to sort through to get the exact information you have.

Here's a radical thought; what if you become the online authority for your company's line of work? The WEB MD of your line of work, so to speak!

The first thought that is likely to pop into your head is why I should do that? And even if you did, what is in it for your business? Wouldn't it be counter-productive, not to mention counter-intuitive to have all the information about your business (including your competitors' information) right there?

"

**Being helpful to customers always helps—
even if it means talking up competitors**

All information is online; customers will
find it anyway. That is why you need to be
the person who helps them out. Collate
all the information and present it to them,
even it means that you are putting yourself
down in some aspects and talking up your
competitors.

Well, I would ask you to pause here and think for just one second. Do you think your customers (or prospective customers) will not find this information if you don't provide it to them? They will! Except it may take them some time and effort.

Let us revisit one of the basic tenets of marketing—customers! They are your starting point and your ultimate destination. When you look it like that, doesn't this exercise make sense?

Okay, let us take a step back and take a look at what a typical marketing journey would look like and why what I am suggesting here makes sense. We will look at it from the customer's point of view and then look at the steps that you need to take to make this journey better so that they will decide to buy your product or service.

The customer journey

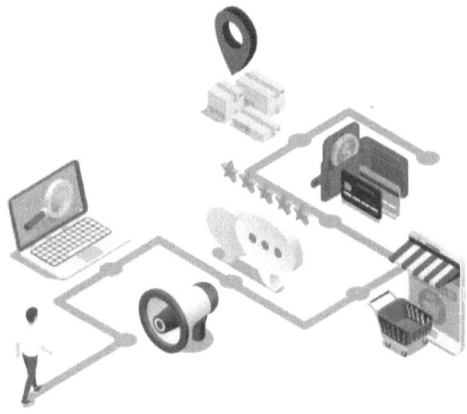

The customer journey, as we all know, starts long before the actual search begins. I am not talking about the basic needs of life like food, shelter, clothing, fuel, and, in today's world, mobile connectivity.

I am talking about other products and services. In that case, we are talking about the primary need-want-longing-like-covet stage. At this stage, the emotion may be there but may not have converted into a tangible requirement. The customer wakes up to the fact that he or she or the business lacks something.

Once that happens, in most cases, the customer knows what they want. If they do not, they seek opinions, look for information to find the product or service that will help them fulfill the need or want they have.

Then starts the buying journey. The customer will start with the options they have. And in today's world, for most products, there are, if anything, too many options. Once they realize that they have choices, customers take a step back.

They list down the criteria they are looking for, which would include many of the specifications but also the price they can afford. Let us take an example to understand how this works.

For the sake of simplicity, let us take a B2C example. A customer hailing from an upper-middle-class family with double income and having a lovely house in the suburbs with a reasonable size garden wants to find a way to ease his aching muscles at the end of the day.

He talks to his friends, colleagues, doctor, and searches for the information online and discovers that a hot-water tub is an excellent way to do that. Once he does some more research, he finds the options he has and how much each one costs.

He will then weigh the pros and cons of each one and put it up against how much he wants to spend and talk it over with this family to get their inputs.

By now, his contact details must be out there in the market, and many hot tub sellers would be reaching out to him with all the information. At this stage, he wants to pause and really dive deeper. He may want to look at

- Which brand, model, and type will help his body aches
- The one which will fit into his budget
- Not cause too much disruption in his household during installation
- Plumbing requirements and energy consumption
- Accommodate his family requirements
- Meet housing regulations
- Other such factors

In the course of his search, he will be touching base with several people—both online and offline. During his journey, he will go through the stages of awareness, consideration, and, finally, decision. The process will be full of intense searches, discussions, and vast amounts of information thrown at him.

Here's what you should do to make the customer journey easier

Continuing with the example, let us assume that you are in the business of selling portable hot tubs that can accommodate 3-4 people and offers 3-5 settings to relax aching muscles.

Now that we have that settled, we are going to say something here that may seem logical and strange at the same time here. Logical, because you are doing some of these things already. Strange, because what we are suggesting may seem weird and counter-intuitive.

List out the options available

Did you know that there are as many as 18 types of hot tubs to choose from? If you did not, there is a chance that the customer may not know either. Become the hot tub authority for your customers and show them their options.

It goes without saying that you may not be in the business of selling some of the hot tub options you are talking about. It does not matter; do list them out.

Talk about cost

Cost is often an ugly subject, and companies do not want to talk about it. But you should. The bottom line is essential, and you are here to sell your product here. Start with the statement that you are here to help them and that you are doing this because you are an expert on the subject and because you want to sell your product to them.

Telling your customers about the cost has a lot of advantages. It can act as the first filter and will eliminate the need to take the customer through the rest of the buyer's journey. And the customer will appreciate your upfront honesty.

The next advantage is that they will have a base to see how you compare with your competition. The customer is also likely to glean the benefits of buying your product and realize that the pricing is right. You are also handing the customer the weapon they need for negotiating on the price.

Make an honest comparison

This is the stage where you become the actual Wikipedia of your product for your customer. Start by putting yourself in your customer's shoes and compare the various types of hot tubs available with their features. Rate them honestly, even it means that you have to openly state that your competitor's product is better than yours in some aspects.

It is entirely acceptable to say that. And I will tell you the reason why. Today most information is available online, and customers are going to find all the details they want.

By being proactive and offering them this information on a platter, you are making a positive impression on your customer. When you treat people right, they will remember you. Even if you are not going to get this deal, the customer will remember the way you provided information.

The next time somebody asks them for related information, they will refer the name of your business, and there is no better publicity than word-of-mouth. The best part is it is free!

What is more, you will slowly but surely gain the reputation of being an authority on this subject. Psst... that is what Google likes too.

Tell them what works and what does not

You have to be upfront about the ways in which your product will work. For instance, the customer wants something stable because of pets and children in his house. He should be able to understand that the movable hot tub will not be stable and that it may not suit his requirements.

You have to remember that the content the customer will look at would be online, which means that you are answering questions that you assume that the customer would have. If anything, answering questions that a typical customer would have during the purchase process is what you have to do.

Make a list of conditions in which your brand of the hot tub would work and, if possible, describe each point in detail. Doing this will ensure that there is no misunderstanding. And if the customer is not fully aware of what he should look for, he would be able to learn that aspect from your content.

Give them a checklist of what they should look for

Sometimes it is not enough to give them something to read but to take it a step further, by giving them something to do. There is something in this for you, too, because you will be gating the content.

When you gate content, customers have to click on your landing page, fill out a form with all the details, to get the asset, which means you get to retain their contact details. In products such as the hot tub, an excellent asset to give them is a checklist of the features that the customer should look for before making the purchase decision.

The advantage here is that you can work to make this asset showcase the good qualities of your product in a subtle manner, while honestly helping the customer at the same time.

Guide them on usage

Who says that the buying journey has to end with the purchase decision? It should not because once the purchase decision is over, there comes the delight phase where customers talk about your products.

In essence, it means that you have a substantial human testimonial that talks about their experience with the product, the buying process, and what they liked about every aspect. Remember? We had talked earlier on about people wanting to buy from humans and not brands.

You can make this happen by staying with the customer even after they have completed the purchase by telling them about the best practices on using the product.

With most products, there is a period (some long, some short) where customers have to use your product. Here is another chance for your company or brand to shine. It is time to show your caring side and also your depth of knowledge by helping customers get the most from the product they have purchased.

Make it easy for your customers to find all the information

Well, now you have worked on a lot of information that will be useful to the customer throughout his or her buying journey. But is that enough? No! You need to make sure that the content you have created is accessible.

At this juncture, you need to start applying SEO (search engine optimization) tactics, and while there is no hack to make it easier, it is not that difficult either. The starting point would be to determine what kind of questions (yes, it is questions rather than simple keywords due to more customers doing a voice search on their mobile device) that a customer is likely to ask.

Once you spend a bit of time doing that, you will know where to start. Start by making those search queries your content titles. It may not always be easy to do it to match word-by-word, but as long as you get the gist right, it should work.

If possible, use numbers in your title to grab the readers' attention. The psychology behind this is that people like to know that they have to do a finite number of things or understand a particular number of factors to get the results they want.

Socialize your content and have your teams share it on their accounts on social media to spread the word. These are just some of the necessary steps that you need to start with. SEO is a vast subject that requires some expert insights to get right. However, you should definitely start building the foundation for the experts to take it to the next level.

The conclusion here is that you need to be sincere in your intentions to help the customer, but you also need to be smart at the same time. One does not exclude the other. When you think of the best buying experiences you have had in your adult life, you will realize that most of them have been a combination of sincere and smart efforts.

Test your knowledge with this simple test

13. When does the customer's purchase journey start?

    a. When they see others having something they have always coveted
    b. When the need strikes them as an urgent requirement
    c. When they feel they can go beyond fulfilling a need to things they want
    d. All of the above

14. How can you help customers make the right purchase decision?

    a. Bombard them with information on how great your product is and promise them it will meet all their requirements
    b. Offer substantial discounts to tempt them to buy your product even though it does not meet most of the criteria that the customer wants
    c. Become the authority on the product and offer them the various choices that he or she has and be honest about the features of your product
    d. Tell them that the rest of the products in the market are inferior and that your product can be adjusted to meet all their needs

15. What aspects of cost and features should you discuss?

    a. Be secretive about cost and do not reveal all the details till the last minute

    b. Pretend that you are there only to help them and not make a sale and tell them bad aspects of your competitor's pricing

    c. Be honest about your intentions and talk about the amount your customer will have to spend and what he or she will get in return

    d. Keep leading them away from the topic of cost and pricing till the last moment so that they have no choice but to buy your product

Make a Huge Effort, Document it, and Showcase it

"Modesty, diffidence, and being reserved are good qualities, but only in personal relationships, not when it comes to marketing."

I will reiterate it again; marketing is not for the timid and self-conscious, at least not when it comes to how you project your brand, product, and company to your customers. That does not mean that reserved and modest people cannot make a place for themselves in the world of marketing or that they cannot be good marketers.

What it means is that while being sincere and focused on your efforts for your customers is vital, it is even more important to showcase it. Showing them what you are doing for them, telling them what measures you are willing to take for them, and the extent to which your brand is stretching to deliver the product or service matters a lot.

"

Make a huge effort, document it, and showcase it

Marketing is a lot of perspiration with a little inspiration thrown in. Why not use this to your advantage? Since the market is more interested in the persona or the person behind the company, document the efforts you make, and showcase it.

Why do you need to make an effort?

If you are a millennial, you probably don't know what it feels like to do without something just because it is not local or seasonal. We are a global village today, where what you desire is flown, acquired, or shipped to ensure that you get it and that too in an immaculate state.

Today, we are used to opening our laptops or mobile devices, surf online, and order what we want. Alternatively, if you are not into delayed gratification (in instances where immediate or two-hour or overnight delivery is not available), we can just walk, drive, or take a cab to the nearest shop to get what we want.

The only factor that could be a hindrance to what you want is the lack of money. But you can even overcome the lack of cash by using a credit card or availing an instant loan (another factor that has become easier to get) so that you can acquire what your heart desires.

The bottom line here is that today, most of the things that we want are easy enough to get. This means that while we enjoy this aspect, we do not value anything we get because it is so easy to get.

By now, you must be wondering what all this has to do with marketing. However, if you introspect a bit more, you will realize what I mean. Let me give you an example to make it clearer.

We are sure many of you drink coffee. Though slightly bitter, it has a rich flavor, not to mention fantastic taste. It is invigorating, refreshing, and comes in many forms. You can take it black or have it with foamy milk, add chocolate, chili powder, salt, etc.

The possibilities of how you consume the beverage are endless. The cost of coffee varies according to the brand, the source, and the kind of processing it goes through.

Have you heard of Black Ivory Coffee or elephant poop coffee? We are sure most of you have. It is made from coffee beans that have literally passed through an elephant's digestive system.

There are many stories around this coffee, which is supposed to taste exquisite. Obviously, the coffee requires a lot of effort to process, given that it has to be fed to elephants and then collected from the pachyderm's excreta to be processed further. The process seems to be complicated and also has some inherent risks.

For the queasy-stomached among us, the thought of drinking something that has been pooped out by an animal (however much we love our elephant friends) is enough to put us off. However, there are still takers of this really expensive coffee. Why do you think that is so?

Yes, the taste and flavor of the coffee is a big part of it, but it is also the tag of exclusivity that makes it even more desirable. People like to think that they are privileged enough to consume something that takes a lot of effort.

In a world where most things are easy to get and use, something that is hard to come by and requires so much effort becomes attractive. By now, you must have grasped what I am trying to tell you.

Yes, customers want to know what they are getting from you is worth it. That you have put in efforts to deliver the product or service that you are selling. In marketing, this is a valuable lesson, because it shows the value of not merely putting in the effort, but also showing what you have done.

There is a subtle difference between a product that has snob or prestige value or something that requires effort. The difference between the two is that the first one shows that you have money (and hopefully good taste), but the second one denotes that you are unusual, you have quirks, and that you are discerning.

Now that we have established that why showcasing your efforts is essential, it is time to look at how you can do it.

Here are some of the options that allow you to do that from the marketing point of view:

Market the journey along with your product or service

We know that customers tend to enjoy those products or services, which suggests that they are hard to get or those that require a lot of effort to create.

Most products or services that you are going to market have some kind of effort that your company has gone through to build. Why not simply ensure that you market the journey that the product or service has gone through along with the product or service itself?

Doing this will automatically have your prospective customers add more value to the product. Let us look at a simple example here. Let us assume that you, the reader, are looking for a lamp to use when you work or read at night.

You have narrowed your choices to two lamps, which meet your required parameters. One of them is marketed as the result of a long-drawn process of product development that the CEO of the company has gone through because her daughter had eyesight issues due to poor lighting. And the other one is a good lamp. The price difference between the two products is not too much.

You are likely to be attracted more to the study lamp with the back story rather than the other one. Right? That is what I am talking about! The next time you are going through a brainstorming session for your marketing plan, try to delve deeper into the journey that your product has gone through and add it as a part of the marketing efforts that you do.

Even if you don't want this to be part of the advertisements, you can put them on social media. This way, you can create a human interest story.

Create videos and collages to showcase the journey

One of the ways to ensure that you have enough material to put out there is by recording the journey in the form of images and videos. However, this may not always be possible, because, in most instances, you may become part of the marketing efforts much later into the journey.

That does not matter. All you need to do is learn about the details and try to use it to the best possible extent in the marketing campaigns that you launch. Not all stories of product or service development will be interesting or have an emotional element, and you may often find yourself adding some features to it.

Let us again look at an example. This time, let us make it difficult and talk about a B2B product, which is usually a tougher market to crack. Take, for instance, software that is used to track human resources like Workday.

Workday is a central software that will help you track your staff, the roles they play, attendance management, payroll, separation, and more. It is supposed to provide you with a single source of truth for all matters related to human resources. You can build up the story for this by digging deeper into the problems that the customers of the product face.

For instance, you can talk about the pricing and finance-related issues that a company faced because they could not account for the teams working at each location. As a result, they ended up billing less to the client, and this resulted in losses. This company (your customer) decided that they wanted a secure and robust means to track their personnel.

They approached your company, who is into software application development and thus was born the product—HRReal. HRReal is not an actual product but something that I have come up with here to use as an example.

You can create this whole journey visually through videos and collages that you can use for your marketing purposes.

Weave bits and pieces in every marketing collateral

Now that you have crafted a story or discovered one, and created the marketing material for it, you can be smart and use it for different marketing collateral. The key is not to go overboard with the story and create pathos but to present it in a very wry, humorous, yet human manner.

Long-drawn stories that go back to the past may not interest most of your customers, who are likely to be millennials. You need to slice and dice the creatives in such a way that they are easy to consume. Before you launch your campaigns, it would be a good idea to have a robust buyer persona in place, along with demographic profiling.

Doing this will help you use your marketing material better. For instance, the slightly mature audience may have more patience while the younger crowd would want to be served everything in a fast and easy manner.

When you are profiling your persona, you may be forced to stereotype certain aspects, but that cannot be helped. The important thing to remember is that you do not talk blatantly outside of your office about this.

If you are bold enough, make your marketing different

Now that you have your product or service development marketing material in place, it is time to decide on how to market it. You can go the conventional way, and place the content in the way your persona would like it on the channel the persona is most likely to go to.

This is a safe and straightforward way to do. For instance, the product you are marketing is a lipstick that is organically sourced and produced using the best ingredients from stellar sources. You have priced the lipstick on the higher side.

The persona you are probably aiming for is the conscientious professional woman in her early thirties. She is attractive, smart, and very aware. She wants to look good, but only if the product is produced ethically. She wants quality and would be willing to pay for it.

You can market this product in journals that professional women are likely to read, on social media that supports visuals more, and also in high-end fashion sites. You can also consider putting it up in education-related women's journals because women who can afford this could also be full-time homemakers who are stay-at-home moms. They are mature, smart, attractive, affluent, and socially conscious.

We are talking about the safe approach here. If you want to make a splash, then you could probably do a campaign asking women to pre-book the lipstick and offer to customize the shade that will best suit them.

This is a bit off from the conventional method but could pay in the long-run.

Most important of all, have your marketing team believe in it

No story, marketing campaign, marketing approach, or strategy would work if you and your team did not believe in it. Your marketing team should completely buy into the concept and the product.

There's an ancient saying that says, you cannot sell a product you don't believe in. What it means that if you are not able to sell it to yourself and your team, then you will not be able to convince your audience.

How can you sell your story to your organization? There is no simple or straightforward way to do this. However, one of the best ways to move this forward is by involving everyone in the nascent stage of the campaign. People tend to love their babies (in this case, the product or service backstory and marketing campaign) no matter how different it is.

Once you have your current team convinced and sold on the concept, it will be easier to convince your audience and the subsequent teams that would work on the marketing campaigns. It is vital that you tell them what you are trying to do, why it is crucial to the whole exercise, and how they can contribute to it.

Once you have their confidence, then seek the team's inputs or feedback as the case may be. If you have anybody in the group who fits in with the demographics of your buyer persona, then make them central to the concept. Encourage them to talk to their peers, collect inputs, and share it with the rest of the team.

Make sure that you take into consideration all the objections and arguments that come your way. Often, these provide the best twists and quirks that your campaign needs to make it a success.

Test your knowledge with this simple test

16. What techniques do you need to use to add a tag of exclusivity to your product or service?

    a. Show the efforts that have gone into creating it, and the various steps involved, price it right and showcase the value

    b. Price it high and make it really difficult to find and buy so that people conclude that there is some hidden value there

    c. Just look at the way your competitors have priced their products and add a hefty mark-up to make it look expensive and thereby exclusive

    d. Launch an exuberant and attractive advertising campaign along with top models and celebrities to up the price and make it look expensive

17. What role can the story of your product development play in marketing?

    a. It is good fodder for gossiping and you can entertain your peers with this story

    b. It can build value and human interest in the way your product was built and help attract leads

    c. It is a waste of time; customers only care about the way the salesperson talks to them

    d. You can use the story to convince people of the quality when your product fails to deliver

18. How important is it for your marketing team to believe in the concept they are selling?

   a. It does not matter at all as long as you can make your visuals pretty and copy interesting

   b. It is integral to the success of your marketing efforts as it lends your campaign with a solid base

   c. Just ask your team to do what you, as a marketing leader think is right, and the results will be good

   d. It is extremely old-fashioned to ask your team to buy in to your marketing ideas and concept

07 Go for the Big Gestures and Don't Worry Too Much Elegance

"Start where you can, study where it leads, and keep going, or else you might as well be moving backward."

When you go out shopping, do you like the surprise freebie? This is a no-brainer; of course, we all love our surprises. We love it when we get that something extra, and this makes us smile all the time. More importantly, for marketers, it makes us go back to that brand in the hope of another such surprise. Once again, it all comes down to what you made a person feel, not what we said or gave.

What does this mean in terms of your marketing strategy? As a company that is struggling with a small marketing budget, many start-ups do not know what they can afford

Go for the big gestures and don't worry too much elegance

When you are just stepping into the market, it is about standing out, and having a suave and elegant personality may not always be the best way. Go for the big and even ostentatious gestures to get noticed.

to give away. Companies do not go for the extra bits because they feel it needs to be classy and elegant. When it comes down to it, elegance is not what most customers seek unless you are in the business of luxury goods.

All you need to do is make it big and bring that special feeling. Let us take a step back and see how you can make a big gesture that does not add too much to your expenses.

This is yet another one of those instances where I will be able to explain better with examples.

Upgrade to the next level

If you are in the business where your customers come back frequently to avail of the service (cab, salon services, etc.) or purchase the product (coffee, fast food, etc.), it is easy enough to throw in an upgrade once in a while.

Have you ever booked a cab and been told that you will get a bigger car but at the same rate? If that has happened to you, you will know that it is indeed a great feeling.

But in terms of marketing, you should take it to the next level by making it big. You can seek the customer's permission to click a picture and share it on social media and even request the customer to do the same thing.

Have a hashtag created for such shares on social media to make it easier to search. Once you have enough of these testimonials and shares on social media, put them together in an animated format and share.

The best aspect of doing this is that it does not need too much effort. In fact, the more rough and ready your content (words and pictures) is, the more natural it will look.

Among the many positive outcomes of such gestures is that more people will be driven to avail of your services or buy your products so that they can enjoy the same extras and the publicity.

Say it with a card

Sometimes, stepping back in time can be the way forward. Invest in some cards that have short, sweet, and pithy messages on it and have your customer-facing teams hand it out. But do make sure that they do it with a lot of discretion so that what is written on the card suits the occasion.

Once again, make it big, and ensure that you record what you are doing and share as deemed apt. Millennials today are not aware of the practice of exchanging cards with personal messages on it, unlike the earlier generations.

So, I will ask you to do this kind of promotional activity with care. Start slowly to see how people react before taking it forward. Whether this activity should be part of your marketing efforts also depends on the product that you are trying to sell.

Smile or shake hands

Another simple yet effective way to create a signature of your product or service in the market is by training your staff to behave in a particular manner. However, the caution here is that you have to consider the cultural factors even as you train the team on what they need to do.

For instance, in some of the more conservative countries, it would be considered rude or forward for a person to shake hands with the opposite gender, while in others, it is the norm to casually hug and kiss each other.

Do take these factors into consideration before you establish a particular protocol associated with your brand. For instance, you can have your customer-facing team always greet people with a specific term.

Or your signature move can be to offer a small toy to every kid who comes to your outlets or offer a flower to women who come to your offices or shops.

This is one of the ways the well-known fast-food brand McDonald's keeps customers coming back for more. Their happy meals had kids clamoring for the toys they got, and soon they were collecting a set.

Add a little extra

Another simple promotional technique that many companies have used successfully is to add that little bit extra. But you can tweak it a bit and offer the extra without announcing it beforehand to create a small surprise element.

However, it goes without saying that when you do this, you need to record it in some way so that you can use it on social media. Have a couple of customers open their packages and record candid reactions to use on social media.

Use those details

When you talk to customers (when they call in, or you call them), use the details you have about them to personalize the interaction. For instance, you realize that the customer's birthday is coming up or if their spouse's birthday is coming up, slip it naturally into the conversation.

But a caution here is that you need to train your customer-facing teams to develop an antenna on when to carry out a lengthier conversation and when to keep it short and crisp.

Sometimes, customers are just looking for a quick and easy fix and do not want to spend too much time talking about other things. In some instances, the customer may be more receptive to talking once their problem has been resolved.

In recent times, people have been inundated with requests for feedback on their interactions with the customer care teams. While this can be an excellent way to discover what customers feel, in some instances, it can become an irritant.

Encourage and acknowledge

When your customer buys something from you (Example: DIY for B2C customers and wind turbine for B2B), follow it up with questions on how well it is working out for them.

For instance, if you are in the business of selling embroidery kits, ask customers how their projects have turned up and request them to see if they would be willing to post a photo in social media and tag your brand.

In the second instance, build a story of why the customer went for renewable energy and share the details of the impact it has had on their business. Share the story on social media congratulating them on how well they are doing. The focus should be on the customer, your brand story should only be incidental.

Be sure to recognize those instances where all that would work are the big gestures and go for it with gusto. There is a place for elegance, and there is a place for vast promotions. The apt marketing strategy would mean recognizing what is required at a particular point in time and going for it.

Always keep your brand and the limitations of your marketing budget to ensure that you get the maximum out of any situation.

Test your knowledge with this simple test

19. What factors should you keep in mind while going for those extras?

    a. Do what comes to mind as spontaneity adds a lot of value to any occasion
    b. Plan according to the product, culture, occasion, and use your discretion to do this
    c. Tell your people to use these gestures when they feel that they have no other option
    d. Use a numerical system to determine when you can add these extra features

20. Why do you need to share customer success stories online?

    a. To show how well your customers like you
    b. To showcase what works and what doesn't
    c. To ensure that you keep building on credibility and goodwill for your brand
    d. All of the above

21. Why do the little extras and special treatments matter a lot in marketing?

    a. It shows that you care and displays the depth of understanding you have about the customer's needs
    b. It is a good way to distract people from the weaker aspects of your products and services

c. Your competition will feel insecure and offer more discounts and end up making a loss

d. It is all about pretending to care about customers so that you can keep selling them bad products

"Building your brand can be a bit like democracy. Build it by the people for people to buy."

Do you believe that brands have a personality? Yes, they do, if you are able to build your brand personality carefully. I don't know how many of you are aware of the way the brand Eureka Forbes created its brand identity during the late eighties and early nineties. When it was newly launched, they were the epitome of their people assuming the brand personality.

"

Have your people become your brand personality

We can all agree that brands have personalities. One of the best marketing hacks is to have your people become your brand personality and that too online. Ask them to use brand-related language and content, even on personal posts.

This brand that used to sell vacuum cleaners (a relatively new concept at that time) adopted the direct selling strategy. They had an army of well-trained young men (mostly men) who would go from one home to another, demonstrating the product. The Eureka Forbes salesforce was known for never taking no for an answer.

They would approach building societies, security guards, and dodge guard dogs to go to homes and insist that people hear them out. More often than not, they would walk out with at least 30% of the people in that locality booking their product. The mix of aggression, vulnerability, and brash friendliness became synonymous with the brand.

Once they had a customer booking their product in the locality, they had no compunction leveraging it to make another sale. Of course, we are talking about an era before cellphones, easy internet access, and social media.

It was an era where many households were proud of a clean home and the fact that they had the latest gadgets. The Eureka Forbes salesforce used this aspect to push forth with their sales. It was not unusual for a housewife to befriend the salesperson and do some selling on his or her behalf.

The brand and the people who were part of the brand became one cohesive personality to sweep (literally and figuratively) the market.

Another brand that has made its people become a part of their brand personality is Lufthansa Airlines. Courtesy is the keyword they have adopted and ensured that every one of their staff behaves according to a specific set of rules. Loyalists of the airlines vouch for their remarkable service and comfort levels.

So, let us look at how you can make your people become part of your brand personality.

The starting point of this exercise will have to be a definition of your brand personality. Even before you do that, you need to define your brand purpose. According to Simon Sinek, knowing why your brand does what it does is the core of your brand definition.

Before it gets confusing, let us look at the logical steps that you need to follow to get your brand personality right.

Start by defining what you do

It is all good to talk about your brand identity, but that will only work if you know what you do. Most companies start out thinking that this is the easy part to do. For instance, Mac cosmetics would say that they sell cosmetics. But wait a minute, is that all?

Once you have defined what you do in such a narrow manner, you are probably restricting yourself to that alone. Let us expand what a company does a bit more. In this example, while Mac is a premium makeup and cosmetics brand, it goes beyond that. It sells women the means to look even more attractive than they are. Is that all?

Actually, you can expand the scope a bit because Mac also sells fragrances. So makeup and fragrances, is that it? No, you can go as far as to say that Mac sells cosmetics that do not harm the skin. Does it mean that they sell good-quality cosmetics and fragrances?

Actually, Mac sells beauty products, skincare products, makeup tools, and perfumes. The key focus here is the word 'beauty' and how Mac helps enhance that. When you broaden the scope of your brand to beauty instead of just cosmetics and fragrances, then you can focus on building a better brand personality but without diluting on the core focus.

This is the exercise you need to undertake along with your team. For instance, if you are in the business of selling cars, a better way of defining your business would be selling personal transportation vehicles as opposed to goods transportation vehicles.

Here are some tips to determine what your brand does:

- Start with the specifics
- Define what aspirations you aim to meet (look better, drive comfortably, etc.)

- Then widen the scope of your products to include that
- Leave scope for logical expansion to other related products without diluting the brand
- Write it down and discuss with a group of people
- Agree on the 'what' aspect of your brand

Come up with key adjectives to define your brand

The definition of what your brand does is just the first step. The next step is to identify the essential qualities that you want to imbue in your brand.

Let us take an example again to understand how to do this. In this case, let us look at a brand that is well-known for its quality—Apple. The brand is known for its quality products that all of us want to own. Whether it is their cellphones, tablets, or laptops, we want them.

Some of the adjectives you would use to define the brand include sterling quality, pricey, value for money, different technology, stability, awesome user experience, to name just a few. Yes, they have certain limitations and restrictions, but we are willing to accept them because the quality of Apple products is excellent.

Now, the question is, what would you like your brand to be known for? Before you start with quality and value for money, let me tell you, those are hygiene factors, and customers automatically expect that. What you need are characteristics that go beyond good quality and pricing.

One of the most beloved brands in India, Amul, has a very distinct brand personality. They use a mix of humor and current headlines to define their brand. It is warm and quirky. Though the brand is about quality food products, people look for the banners and promotional content the brand puts out just to see what they have come up with.

Steps you need to take to define the key adjectives that describe your brand:

- Ask everyone in your team to write down three aspects that make them proud to be working for their brand
- Then ask them to define why they are proud of the three points that they just wrote down
- Pull out adjectives from the above and categorize them in three buckets according to their commonality
- Finalize the three main attributes that you want to use to define your brand

Develop the customer persona you are targeting for

While you are in the process of identifying and establishing your brand personality and imbuing your team with this personality, don't forget your customer. Doing this is essential because the customer is an integral part of the marketing jigsaw, and without the customer, the whole exercise may be pointless.

CUSTOMER PERSONA

The correlation between your brand personality and customer persona is like the body type you have and the clothing you wear. It has to fit, or else it becomes an exercise in futility.

Let us take another example to make it easier. Can you imagine a person in his eighties going for a brand like Forever 21? As a rule, this may not happen that often, though there could be exceptions. This is why you need to define and develop the kind of customer persona you are aiming for with your brand personality.

When you are defining your customer persona, go with the average and not the exceptions. For instance, you have a person in their nineties rocking spandex outfits. This could come under the exception category. Draw a word picture of what you envision your target customer to be like.

He or she can even have characteristics like conservative, new-age, quirky, fashionable, smart, number-oriented, logical, artistic, etc., apart from the usual demographics that we have.

For instance, if you have visited Etsy, it caters to a crowd that appreciates the handmade, vintage, craftsy stuff rather than the mass-produced products. Just think how Etsy would have defined their customer persona as opposed to how Amazon would have done it, and you will head in the right direction.

If you are thinking more in terms of B2B, then look at how a Siemens (a technology company) would define their customer persona versus how Vestas RRB (a wind turbine manufacturer) would identify theirs. And you have a gist of what you need to add and how to build a persona for your potential customer.

Pick a tone that will work long-term for you

The tone of voice that your brand plans to use is something that will have to adopted by your team as well. For instance, the tone of voice that Nike has is to say that you can do anything, and their defining statement is 'impossible is nothing' which makes you think and be inspired.

The brand goes on to encourage you to push your limits in search of health and fitness. The tone and tagline can be seen in all their brand material, and they have used it effectively.

Another brand that comes to mind is Tata Steel. Their tone is a do-gooder who does a lot of social work, develops underdeveloped areas, encourages those underprivileged to come up, and other such things. Their tagline used to be ' We also make steel.'

With changing times, they have updated this to 'Values stronger than steel,' which is in keeping with their core belief and value system.

How do you define your tone of voice?

- Meld the brand personality and customer persona to write down the main features that stand out
- Come up with strong qualities that will denote your brand

- Balance these qualities with a softer aspect like courage, compassion, determination, ecologically aware, etc.
- Try it out on a target group of people to assess their reaction about your tone of voice
- Write down why you have defined the tone of your voice the way you have. Read it back to see if it makes sense
- Tweak it if required and ensure that it is a broad range that can be used over the long-term

Give it a verbal and visual identity and write down how, when, and why of your brand

Once you have the personality aspect, the tone of voice down for your brand, you need to work on the look and feel of your brand. This will further solidify your identity and ensure that people can immediately relate to your brand. Remember the apple with a bite out of it used by Apple? It is a simple enough thing, but it is known the world over.

Start by defining the colors that your brand will use, the fonts that you can and cannot use, have a logo in place, and ensure that you have guidelines on how to use it. Make sure that you have imagery themes, a list of dos, and don'ts for the kind of videography and pictures that your brand can use.

If your brand has a tagline or a brand promise, define how it can be changed or modified as per the situation. You can also put in content and style guidelines in place to ensure that any visual or written material that comes out of your company is strictly according to the brand personality.

While defining the brand personality, tone of voice, setting the colors, the fonts, the design themes, etc. is essential, it is equally important to document it.

Documenting the how, the when, and the why aspects of your brand will ensure that your entire team is aware of the direction they need to take. In any organization, there is bound to change with people leaving and others joining, and you do not want to depend on the memory of a few people to carry the brand personality forward.

Write down the vision (what you see your brand as), the mission (what your brand is planning to do), and the purpose statement (why it is going to be doing this).

To ensure that your people take on your brand personality, make sure that you take each and every existing team member and, after that, the new member of the team through the brand guidelines. If possible, create a course that they can take it up and get certified.

Gamification of your brand-related content can make it easier to consume and remember. You can go a step deeper and create guidelines for every customer interaction or touchpoint that your team is likely to have to ensure that your people really represent the brand personality.

Test your knowledge with this simple test

22. How do you build a brand identity, starting with what you do?

    a. Start with the specifics, define what it does, broaden the scope, and aspirational value

    b. Create a complex product guide that will tell you how and when the product was conceived and created

    c. Make sure that you do not use vague language and narrow it down only to the specifics

    d. Just leave it to the production folks; they know what they are doing

23. What is the correlation between brand identity and customer persona?

    a. It is the connection between the product and the production process

    b. It is similar to the connection to the body type you and the clothing that will work for it

    c. The connection is like flight schedules that tie into each other

    d. It is about pairing socks; they should be a perfect match

24. How do you ensure that everyone in your company has an idea of brand personality?

   a. Just let them figure out by going through the brochures and other content you have
   b. Let them come up with their own version so that they have the satisfaction of doing it
   c. There is no need to do this because your brand is so strong that people will anyway identify it
   d. Discuss, debate, and formalize this so that you can share it as part of the onboarding process

09 Give it Away for Free or With a Massive Discount if You Can Capitalize on Your Customer

"The best sales happen when you get your customers to do the selling."

The saying that you have to give something to get something applies here. But the caveat is that you have to be strategic in what you give away, how you give it away, and to whom you give it away. Moreover, the giveaway trick may not work for every product and service.

Why would anybody want to give away their product or service away for free? Just think again. Many companies have been doing this, and they do this for an excellent reason. It all comes down to publicity. Yes, publicity, the indefinable aspect that every celebrity both seeks and avoids.

Why does the free giveaway or discount trick work?

It is simple; we all look up to somebody or at least the image that somebody has cultivated as their public persona. We

“

Give it away for free or with a massive discount if you can capitalize on your customer

If you can get a public personality to endorse your product or service, do it even it means that you give your product or service away.

look up to Bill Gates not only for his genius in setting up Microsoft but also for the charity works he does.

We look up to celebrities not just because we admire them and idolize them but also for aspirational reasons. When you look at people who have made it big in life, you want to be like them. What is more, when you hear their life stories, you feel that they have gone through struggles like anybody else, and made mistakes before they reach the place they have.

It is all about aspiring to be like them. We are curious to learn about your favorite celebrity's habits, likes, lifestyle, dislikes, etc. What does this have to do about marketing? Actually, everything!

It all starts with building a brand that causes a lot of emotion in you. You need to start your marketing with some kind of emotions to build that people-to-people bond that is essential for a person to make a buying decision. While not every purchase has a long process to arrive at a decision, there is always some form of emotion involved in the process.

As a marketer, your goal should be to touch or tap on that emotional core and spur your customer to make a purchase decision, which favors your product or service. One of the hacks to do that is by using a celebrity for kindling that emotion.

BUYING DECISIONS ARE ONLY 20% LOGIC & 80% EMOTIONAL

Here are some ways in which you can reach out to tap on the emotions of the buyer with the help of this hack. No matter what your business is—B2C or B2B—one of these will fit into the celebrity that you should rope in to bring out the right feeling in your potential customers. Let us take a look at the many different types of stars that you can tap on which one will work for which product or service.

The macho celebrity

The guys want to be him, while the girls want their partner to be like him. This celebrity can endorse anything, and you will have the younger generation and even some of the older generation buying that product.

Take, for instance, James Bond, the man is good-looking, he has the best gadgets, he wears a suit no matter what the situation, and manages to kill baddies without losing any limbs. We know James Bond is a character, but if the actor playing the role were to say that he used a cologne, then most of the population would want to buy it.

Getting the celebrity to endorse your product will be expensive, but you can offer somebody similar, a freebie, and click a picture to use on social media. You can even take it another step forward and run a contest for people to pose like a macho celebrity, give them products (either free or at a substantial discount), click pictures, and post them online.

The gorgeous diva

These are the beauties who seem too good to be true. Ideal for cosmetics, clothing, cars, and well, many other things, it is again a difficult task for you to get them onboard to be seen using and endorsing your product.

One of the ways many companies have managed to make this happen is paying them one-time to do an appearance and be seen holding the product to use it for several promotions.

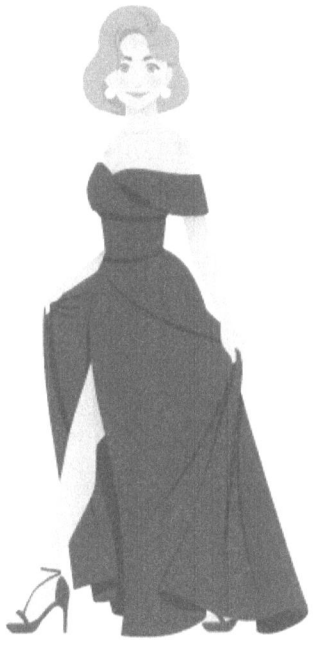

However, many among us are not that big a star but still famous in their own way. Take, for instance, beauty bloggers. They have a following of their own and an enviable reach. You can offer them a voucher that they can spend in your store or website on the condition that they blog about it, complete with pictures.

Here are some of the ways to work around this situation:

- Offer a free coupon (as mentioned here)
- Sponsor a goodie basket to the star

- Approach on social media to get a mention
- Ask them to blog about you
- Build up a likeness competition

The quintessential family man

There are some celebrities out there who are considered the quintessential family man or woman. Take, for instance, Indira Nooyi, she is the top honcho of PepsiCo and also a self-confessed homebody who loves to spend a lot of time at home.

If you can rope in someone like that to be seen buying a home from your company or a car, you will be able to get a lot of mileage. But once again, the budget may be a significant constraint here. Once again, you may consider somebody relatively well-known who is locally recognizable to do the same thing for you.

The sports sensation

Local gyms are roping in minor and major sports stars to endorse them. You can do something like that for most products, but once again, it can be a costly affair.

The best way to approach this is to make it a one-time thing and make the most of it. Another smart way to approach is to take somebody who is into fitness and build her or him into a celebrity and then use that to promote your brand.

The corporate honcho

These we know and want to emulate if not for anything, but for the smart way, they have grown in what is a tough environment. Surprisingly, these may be the guys who will do a bit of publicity for you as long as the product they are asked to endorse, use, and talk about is classy enough and fits their profile.

You can leverage people with this kind of profile for B2B products as well as some of the high-end B2C products.

From here on, we will look at celebrities that you need to build up and then leverage in your marketing campaigns:

The girl next door phenomenon

Who says the girl-next-door cannot be a hero or a leading lady? We are talking about the regular and turning it into a legend. This would work very well if you build up a story around this person, and the product that she is endorsing is relatively not-glamorous.

Examples could include taking a nurse and making her into a crusader of health by having her use a personal hygiene product or a gardener using organic manure to grow healthier vegetables.

The cute sweetheart

She is the one you want to take back to your mom, the one you see yourself settling with, and the one who will be the adorable mom to your kids. This kind of celebrity profile can endorse anything that requires a lot of heart involved in the purchase like your first home, your furniture, your car, and so on.

The sensible intellectual

Build this character to endorse your stock marketing software or your accounting software. You can pick someone from your own team to build the image for and have them do some publicity for you and that too on social media.

The authentic humanitarian

Your human resources department, more specifically the corporate social responsibility guys, can be roped into doing some posting on your product or service's behalf. Once again, building up their profile and the 'talk' around them will help your cause.

The lovable eccentric

We all have someone like this in our lives; the ones who love chaos, cannot wear clothes that match, who like to dance in the rain (genuinely and regularly), and believe in the weirdest things.

If you need a hint, think of Sheldon from Big Bang Theory, or Phoebe from Friends, or Luna Lovegood from Harry Potter. In most cases, you need to discover the eccentrics, you cannot invent them. After all, being true to yourself and not being shy about takes a different kind of heroism, which is no less valuable than the type of power celebrities brings.

Test your knowledge with this simple test

25. What does celebrity persona have to do with marketing?

    a. It touches upon aspirations people have, and by using a celebrity for publicity, you can relate the product with the aspirations of the buyer
    b. Celebrities have a lot of means to gain publicity themselves, and by attaching your brand to them, you can gain from it
    c. The general public wants to know more about their favorite celebrities and this publicity can help
    d. It has nothing to do with brand value or perception, but just a cheap publicity stunt

26. What is the key to making the celebrity endorsement work for your brand?

    a. It does not matter what choice you make as long as the celebrity is a publicity hog
    b. Always go for a lot of celebrities so that you cannot miss on one of them hitting the nail on the head
    c. Match the product with the personality to ensure that it touches an emotional chord in the customer's minds
    d. All celebrities are equal and you can go with the one you can afford

27. What is the option if you cannot afford to have a celebrity as part of your marketing campaigns?

    a. Just steal some photos and clippings of a celebrity you like and use these for marketing purposes
    b. Create your own version of a relatable celebrity with smart storytelling and a persona
    c. Ignore any external factors and ensure that the product details look very attractive even if the quality is not good
    d. Boast of celebrities and drop hints without actually presenting the celebrity at any point in your campaign

10

When it Comes to Market Segmentation, Niche it Right

"How will you dish your marketing efforts out if you don't niche your segment right?"

Digital marketing is all about putting the right information about your company and product or service out there with the hope that your potential customer sees it. At least it may seem that way, to many of us. While this is not entirely untrue, it is also not the complete truth.

Then, what is the way you make sure that your marketing efforts collide (in the best possible manner) with the ideal potential customer? By the ideal prospective customer, I mean the one who not only needs your product or service because it meets his or her needs but also is in a position to buy it.

Even reading that sentence may have tired you out because while digital marketing is not rocket science, it is not straightforward either. You need to be smart in the way you approach it. What do I mean by the smart approach to marketing here?

When it comes to market segmentation, niche it right

In marketing, it is all about making a place for yourself in the noisy and often over-crowded marketplace. This could mean that you do not go for a slice of the whole market but rather a small and distinctive niche where your brand can stand out.

The mistake many of us as marketers make is assuming that the market that we are aiming at should be as broad as possible. So, when somebody asks you who is your perfect prospective customer, we often come back with a description that is too broad. What is wrong with that, you ask?

Well, in marketing, you must get your customer profiling right even before you finetune your product or service. If you remember, something that the wise marketing guru, Philip Kotler, said. He said that marketing starts and ends with the customer. It does not matter that marketing has moved almost entirely to the digital world, the basic principles still apply.

Let us take a deeper dive into the marketing ocean to look at the following aspects:

- What happens when your segmentation is too broad?
- What should be part of your customer persona?

- How do you niche it right when it comes to marketing?
- Why niching will bring better results and save on costs?

What happens when your segmentation is too broad?

In the digital marketing world, whether your efforts are organic, paid, or ideally the right mix of two, you will need to spend time, money, and efforts to make it effective.

Let us start by looking at an example. But before we do that, you have to remember that you have to go by the rule and not the exception.

The example: Let us assume you are in the business of selling cloth manufacturing machines that convert jute into naturally silky and luxurious fabric. Your marketing niche would ideally be those who would be supplying such fabric to designers who are known to use luxurious and natural fabrics in their creations.

Does this mean that any cloth manufacturer across the country will be your customer? Not necessarily. Jute is a raw material that is available in certain places, and it is good sense to assume that a manufacturer who is located in areas where access to jute is plentiful and economical would be the right customer segment to aim for.

So, here we are looking at manufacturers who supply to designers and have access to jute is the segment. Is that enough? Not really. You need a manufacturer who wants to work with jute and not go for a cheaper and easier to manufacture synthetic fabric, which has a bigger market with most apparel manufacturers.

The segmentation would be manufacturers:

- Who is willing to invest in machinery that lets them mill jute into rich and silky material
- An interest in natural fabrics, even if they are more expensive to manufacture
- With an ability to seek out designers who will use the fabric in their designs.
- Cloth manufacturers who plan to use the fabric themselves to launch a new line of clothing
- Manufacturers who have found an export market for this kind of clothing

In case you have not considered the above and other related factors, then you will probably be targeting your organic and paid efforts towards all cloth manufacturers.

If you do not realize what is wrong with doing this, then let me tell you some of the factors that could go horribly wrong, resulting in poor marketing results and loss of reputation.

When you are marketing online, your reputation and standing are especially important, and when you lead the wrong type of customer through the buying journey, this can result in loss of face. It will make your efforts look wrong and, in some instances, fraudulent. And once customers decide that you do not have the capacity to deliver on your promises, they would firmly put you in the not-to-go-to category.

Apart from the loss of face, the essential factor to focus is that you will not be reaching the customer section that fits in with your product, which is the point of your marketing campaign in the first place.

What is the use of getting customers who want to produce polyester cloth when what you are selling is a technology that does not aid in that process at all? Or finding yourself having to modify your product to fit customer demands, which can be expensive and not the best strategy?

To sum it up, not niching it right would result in:

- Loss of reputation
- Poor customer experience

- Leads that do not fit your product
- Bad publicity overall
- Wasted marketing efforts and resources

Now that we know why we should be doing a proper niching of our marketing efforts let us move on to the next phase.

What should be part of your customer persona?

Let us take this section with the same example, which is cloth manufacturing machinery that helps transform the raw material, jute into the luxurious fabric.

With such a product, what should be the customer persona be like?

- Your ideal customer should be a current cloth manufacturer who is doing well in his or her business and is looking for plans to expand his or her business
- In terms of demographics, your customer would be young-to-middle-aged, well-to-do, modern in thinking, and relatively well-tuned with the latest trends and fashions
- He or she needs to be well-connected with the fashion world and in tune with the modern trend of moving back to traditional fabrics even if it is more expensive and difficult to produce
- In theory, this persona would be on social media and be in the habit of checking out what works and what does not. He or she is comfortable talking about his or her passion and vision on social media as well as in-person
- He or she has a risk-taking capacity and has access to funds (either own or borrowed) to invest in the project. He or she is aware that the product will need some marketing and are prepared with the resources to do this.
- He or she also has a vision on the next steps of what he or she will do once his or her current vision takes off

From the above example, you will realize that apart from the demographic factors, you will also need to add depth and breadth to your buyer persona with the attitude, likes, resources, approach that your customer is supposed to have, and take. Once you have these details, you will find it easier to work backward on what content and channels will work for this persona.

How do you niche it right when it comes to marketing?

Once it is evident in the minds of your marketing team, who they would like to sell their product to, then it is time to work backward. First and foremost, you have to establish yourself in your customers' minds as a brand that is different.

Now that we have what we see the customer as and what he or she likes, the next step is to convince them that the product you have fits the niche that they want to be in. You know that the customer is discerning. They want to be seen as crusaders rather than followers.

Your ideal customer would like to know that they have gone beyond the usual to make a positive impact. While saving the environment is important to them (that's why the natural fabric), they also want to be profitable (your designer angle), aesthetics matter to them (it has got to be pretty), and sustainable.

Your content has to address these needs they have and ensure that they see you as the partner for them in their journey and not somebody who only wants to make a sale. Often, you know you have hooked the customer when you realize what is their 'ugh' moment and converted that into 'that's what I want' moment.

Your visuals have to strive to have that class and exclusivity that your customers think is their right. Your marketing material should touch upon the commercial, economic, aesthetic, and emotional needs of your customer.

If you want your whole marketing team to use this archetype of the customer as an inspiration and a beacon when they are lost, then it would be a good practice to write details on a board for them to refer to.

Why niching will bring better results and save on costs?

While creating a niche for yourself in the market is essential to ensure that you stand out and appeal to your specific customer persona, it also has many practical benefits.

To start with, you will be able to plan your marketing efforts better. You can begin by removing those elements that are not going to work at all. For instance, in this example, hoardings are not going to work, at least in this niche.

You want something that focuses on your target audience. In this case, you would be better off going for targeted campaigns on visual social media like Pinterest or Instagram. Even in more prominent companies, the marketing budgets have limits and are provided with the understanding that it will be used with prudence and focus on producing immediate results.

Yes, having a focused niche will somewhat limit your reach and reduce the number of potential customers you can focus on. However, on the positive side, it will ensure that you are not shooting blindly in the dark, hoping to hit your target.

Here are the main benefits of niching it right:

Your customer persona will be bang on

One of the most important elements in marketing is understanding your customer better. It is, in fact, the key to everything, including the product, the promotion, the price, and the positioning. When you have your niche right, then you are that much closer to the customer persona, which means you get all the aspects right.

For instance, with some customers, the key is to talk only about the price, but with others, creating a green impact could be more important. In some others, the vital aspect to focus on could be exclusivity and so on.

When you take your niche research and strategy seriously, you will be surprised how much reach you will get for your marketing efforts.

You can expect to reach your audience better

The idea behind the concept of digital marketing is that you reach your audience at the right time. In some instances, even if you are not able to convert your audience into a paying customer, you would want them to be influencers.

As you must be aware, customer personas are different from buyer personas, which is a step deeper. It takes into account the different roles the buyer persona has to play either as the person who makes the decision or the person who is likely to use the product to get ahead in his or her job, or the person or group of people who will use the product.

Your customer persona could be a culmination of all the buyer personas, including the decision-maker, the influencer, and the user or users. Niching it right will enable you to touch upon the points that matter to each of these personas.

Your budgets will produce better results

Budgeting is an aspect of marketing that most of us love to hate. Budgets limit our efforts but also tell you whether you are getting the required return on investment. You need to have a budget and use it well.

When you have your niche in place, you will spend smartly. What might not work for some niches will work for your niche. For instance, when it comes to our example, while it may be expensive to advertise in online and offline fashion publications, it could be the most effective. As opposed to general paid advertisements, this could get you better reach towards the customers who are likely to buy your product.

You will learn the nuances of organic marketing

Even when it comes to organic marketing where you use the content in your webpages, blogs, and other posts to attract customers, you are better off when you have your niche right. Once you have the niche right, you can produce content that will resonate with the audience.

While most consider organic efforts to reach the audience a lesser expensive option, it does have some costs involved—namely, your content, design, SEO, and web automation teams.

Even with an in-house team working on these aspects, it always better to learn the nuances that will work with your niche audience.

You can become an authority in your field

One of the best ways to improve your lead generation, searchability, and reachability of your marketing efforts is to become an authority in your field of work. In effect, people should consider you the equivalent of Wikipedia or equivalent so that you stand out.

When you have the niche right, your whole team can focus on becoming specialists in that niche. They can ensure that your company is recognized as an expert online by Google, which will boost your marketing efforts. You could dive deeper not only into the benefits and disadvantages of the niche, do comparisons, right about price break-ups, and the dos and don'ts to become an authority.

You will waste lesser efforts and save more

When your efforts are focused, you know which section of the audience you want to reach and how you will do it, then you become more efficient. Not only will your efforts become more focused and more result-oriented, but you will also be able to spend wisely and curb unnecessary spending.

Effective marketing requires you to do less and produce more results while saving costs, and getting your niche right will help you do that.

Test your knowledge with this simple test

28. What are the factors to consider when you segment your market as per your product?

   a. Ability to pay, willingness to buy, and access to the next-level consumers along with an understanding of the product potential and the right vision
   b. The capability of investing along with some knowledge of the industry but not sure they really want to go for this particular option
   c. Want to buy but do not have the means to raise funds and does not have any idea about the next steps to realize profits
   d. Has no idea what is involved, but wants to try something new because it sounds interesting

29. Why is identifying the right niche critical?

   a. The right niche will help you become a market leader because there will be less competition and customers will look up to you
   b. It brings focus to marketing, gets better ROI, meets the right customers' needs, and helps build a better brand image
   c. Because without the right niche, it would be difficult to convince the management about your marketing strategy
   d. You will be able to meet and overcome competition and convince customers better

30. What impact does getting the niche right have on your marketing budgets?

    a. The right niche means that only specific customers will look at your ads and this means that you will get a positive impact every time

    b. The right niche will make it impossible for your competitors to penetrate your market segment

    c. Getting the niche right will ensure that your marketing campaigns are more focused and you have a better reach

    d. The right niche will mean there is no need for advertising and that you can simply approach them in person

Be Shameless When it Comes to Using Your Personal and Professional Contacts

11

> "There is a place for being bashful, and marketing is definitely not it."

A lot of people are under the misconception that to be a successful marketer, you need to be an exuberant extrovert. While that could help in some instances, it is not a prerequisite. However, what a successful marketer needs to be is goal-oriented and ruthless in the pursuit of what he or she wants to achieve.

You need to search and use every resource you have when it comes to ensuring that your marketing efforts are hitting the target. If it means letting your personal and professional lives mingle together for the greater good, then so be it.

Many of us hold our personal contacts back, assuming that our personal and professional lives are better off separate. However, in marketing, you never know what aspect of your life will add to the synergy of your efforts and provide unexpectedly exceptional results.

As you read this, you may be confused but read on through this brief chapter to understand the value leveraging your contacts

"

**Be shameless when it comes to using your
personal and professional contacts**

Digital marketing is no place for a shrinking
violet. You need to start networking, making
contacts, and using all your personal and
professional contacts. There is no shame in
doing this blatantly.

can have. Let us dive a bit deeper with an example that may sound negative, but can be effective when harnessed right.

I am going to start by giving you an example of gossip, the one thing that we are all eager (even if secretly) to hear but loathe to be a part of. How does it work? Gossip is probably one of the most compelling examples of marketing where the personal and professional mingle together to spread the message.

However, since gossip does not have a deliberate or well-thought-out strategy supporting it, it could result in distorted results.

Take, for instance, a simple rumor about a colleague that somebody happens to share with a group of 3 people in the office. It is exciting and controversial, so the group of three moves to the cafeteria to discuss it over a cup of coffee. As the three put together their heads to talk about it, two others who are passing by, join the clique.

Soon the group of five disperse to their respective places. They keep recounting the news and are inspired to share it with their spouses, siblings, and friends. The new is intriguing and touches a chord in one of the people who listened to this news, and they decide to post something on social media.

People in their network, read the post, comment on it, and go on to discuss it with their network of personal and professional acquaintances. Before you know it, the news has spread to at least 10000 more people than initially intended and that too without any conscious efforts.

Imagine the power that this kind of reach can have, especially if you plan and make a conscious effort.

I am talking about harnessing the immense power we have but are not aware of just by being social beings. Yes, even those of you who consider yourselves introverts can add yourself to this category.

How do you harness your personal and professional contacts to further your marketing efforts?

Now that we have built a foundation for the need to leverage (why you need to do it), all your contacts to further your marketing efforts, let us look at how you can do it.

We will follow the same route as the gossip mongers but with better intentions and more focus.

Talk about it

If you and your team have worked on a marketing campaign, keep it confidential till you launch it, only if required, or else, you should be talking about it all the time. Talk to the other departments in the company, speak to people at home about it, discuss it with your peers and friends, and put it out on your groups and forums.

Don't let modesty or the fact that others may not find it interesting stop you. In any case, when you talk with passion and conviction, people will listen and will, if you are lucky, talk about it with others.

Just imagine, if you and the other members in your team manage to talk about your marketing efforts with about six people in each of your personal and professional circles. And half of these people talk to their acquaintances, you already have a considerable number of people knowing about it.

You never know who among this circle is an influencer or, better yet, a potential customer.

Share it

Once you have some marketing materials ready and out on your website, blog, and social media, it is time to take your efforts to the next level. Make it a best practice in your team (and their personal and professional circle, if possible) to have them share this information on their social media with a bit added about their efforts in creating the marketing material.

For example, a designer could talk about the techniques and thought processes that went into the creation of a marketing video. While this may seem a bit self-promotional (so what?), it will spark interest in his or her peers, and they will comment on it or at least like it.

When your marketing posts are viewed, liked, commented, and discussed on social media, there is a more significant likelihood of the right person coming across it. What is more, it requires minimal effort and reinforces the belief that people like to buy from other people and not brands.

Social media, forums, and personal shares are all the kind of marketing efforts that bring results without any significant spending.

Highlight it

One of the other ways that you can bring more focus from your personal and professional contacts on the marketing efforts that you and your team are putting in is by highlighting it. Leave no stone unturned and ensure that you highlight the marketing material during company meetings, social gatherings, and on popular sites.

Doing this could mean that you may come across as a boastful group of people, but you will still be noticed and remembered. Another way to effectively highlight your marketing efforts is by sparking off smart and thought-provoking discussions and debates. But I have to tell you that you will have to develop a thick skin when it comes to the trolls and haters.

Comment and discuss

When it comes to marketing, it is not just important to speak and be heard but also to listen to what others are saying. It is all merely a case of being receptive to others so that they will listen to you. Which is why you need to have a presence in other people's shares and opinions.

If anything, you should develop the reputation of a person who reads, understands, and has something to offer. This way, people are more likely to look at what you share. They are more likely to participate in any discussion you have. And if you can bring a personal style to the way you comment and engage in conversations, then more power to you!

Call for inputs

Sometimes, you have to get a discussion going or simply establish a brainstorming session by calling out for inputs. This comes in useful when you don't have time for thinktanks or focus groups. Reach out to your personal and professional contacts and ask them what they think.

You would be pleasantly surprised at the kind of inputs that you are likely to gather and the way these inputs can shape the way forward for you. You can always select the audience for contributions based on the needs of your marketing efforts and then use these inputs to improve the way you message, focus, or share.

Answer questions

Google wants you (or your brand) to be an authority in your area of business. How do you become an expert? It is simple; invite and answer questions. Please note that I said simple, not easy. It will take some doing, but it will be worth the effort. In this, too, harness the power of your personal and professional contacts.

Don't hesitate to have a definite opinion or offer inputs with the inherent caution of not offending anyone, at least intentionally. Be bold and firm in all the questions you answer even if it means that you are sometimes taking the competition's side.

Address concerns

People have problems, and they want to know that others have them too. What is more, they also want solutions or at least ways around these problems.

You and your marketing team can become the source of their solutions, at least in your field of work. For instance, you are in the business of providing housekeeping services; then, you and your team can take up the responsibility of answering cleaning-related questions for your personal and professional circle.

Make it entertaining

While you are out there sharing, answering, commenting, offering and seeking opinions, do not forget to be engaging. All these efforts will only further your marketing cause if you are able to hook your audience and carry them with you.

An element of storytelling, humor, and dramatics is the way to go. However, the usual caution of being politically correct and not offending anyone applies here.

Test your knowledge with this simple test

31. What kind of personality does a marketer need to have?

    a. Brash, outspoken, loud, and disruptive to the extent that people both like them and resent them
    b. Confident, focused, well-organized, numbers-oriented, and strategic in their approach to each task
    c. Timid, shy, and conservative in their approach to any task and usually would like to be ignored
    d. An unusual mix of brash and conservative making them confusing to work with

32. You should never allow your team to talk about the efforts in the creation of marketing assets? Right?

    a. Right, you don't want anybody taking unnecessary credit or sharing the process of creation with the competition or with customers
    b. Wrong! You want your team to feel good about themselves and showcase the process they followed to create marketing materials while harnessing the power of their contacts and social reach once you have launched the campaign

c. Right, it is only fair to cover up the processes you have internally and making sure that the personal and professional lives on social media do not mingle

d. Wrong, you should encourage your team to share on their social media accounts because it will save you the effort of posting it on the company social media pages

33. What should you and your team do once they have shared marketing-related posts on personal social media accounts?

a. They should post provocative comments and make derogatory comments about the competition

b. They should encourage conversations, engage, and answer to comments with a calm and composed manner while sharing the right information

c. You and your team should forget that you shared anything on social media because your role in this ends right there

d. Make sure that you tag people who seem to represent the customer segment you want to target so that their pages are flooded with your posts

12 Start With a Story Even it is Fictional to Get More People to Consume Your Content

"Think about it; whether it is history or a mystery, stories are the lifeline."

Why do you watch soap operas or series? What fascinates us about movies? How does mythology have the power to draw us long after all the characters are gone? When do we start paying attention to what is being said as humans? Where does our mind go when we hear some exciting incidents?

The answer to all the questions above comes down to stories. Stories have the immense power to draw us out of ourselves and be part of another time and place. We love the different reality that stories offer and sometimes seek them as solace from our troubles. Sometimes stories are merely entertainment when the mundane bogs us down.

"

Start with a story even it is fictional to get more people to consume your content

It may be challenging to do this but, come up with a story about why you started your business and capitalize on this in all your marketing campaigns. Make it relatable by adding some angst and suffering to the story.

In some instances, stories are what we relate to because what is happening to us is also incredible, and there is comfort in knowing that we are not alone.

By now, I am sure the question in your mind must be 'What does this have to do marketing?' or 'ah-ha, I know where this is going!' The whole point of this book has been to make marketing more straightforward and more consumable for you, and storytelling is an integral part of the entire narrative.

Think about it. What are your favorite brands? Your recall of brands or products will immediately go to the 'interesting' ones. And how do you define what is interesting? Something that drew you in and held your attention. What drew you in? I am sure it was some story around the brand or the product or the entrepreneur.

Now, you must be thinking, 'I am working in the marketing department of this (fill in the blank) company, and I am not sure they have an exciting story to share. If you are thinking on those lines, I suggest that you read the title of this chapter again.

Yes, I am talking about creating a story if you don't have one. 'Isn't that cheating?' would be your reaction. But then I believe that all is fair in love, war, and marketing. Because marketing is both love and war.

Marketing can be defined as love because it requires intense passion, commitment, and determination to come to fruition. And marketing is war because the competition is intense, and unless you are proactive, bold, well-armed, and prepared to meet and overcome challenges, you have no place in it.

Let us now get down to brass tacks and determine how you can create stories about the products and services you are marketing with ease.

Here are some tips you can use:

You can take the personal route

What makes an entrepreneur tick, how did he or she reach where he or she did? Did they struggle? Did their family support them? Did they ever think of giving it all up? What do they do on a daily basis to become and stay a success?

Do normal emotions affect them? Is your entrepreneur a night owl or an early riser? What does he or she eat? Is the entrepreneur a detail person or an overall picture person? What does he or she do for entertainment?

In most companies, you have a chief promoter who came up with the concept and decided to start the company. You can make this person the hero of your story. You can start a series of 'did you know?' or 'what makes them tick?' to get your story going.

You can take inspiration from J.K.Rowling, the author of the world-famous Harry Potter series. Today, you hear stories about her struggles and how she feels guilty about spending money, and so on.

There is no doubt that her stories are based on fact, and they are interesting because she showed us imagination and persistence will flourish even if you are struggling for survival and have to deal with depression, among many other problems.

Even today, people lap up stories about her life and the account of how she had to fight so many factors and face so many struggles to achieve what she did.

It can start with a problem that you solved

I don't know if you have heard this story, but it always fascinated me. The story of how the ice cream cone was born. Apparently, there was an ice cream vendor who would sell cups of ice cream at a park and would be frustrated with the litter that he would have to clear up at the end of the evening as people would throw their used cups when they ate the ice cream.

One day as he was clearing the cups at the end of a tiring day, he thought to himself, "I wish people would eat the cup as well! Then I would not have to clear up." And that thought sparked the idea of edible cups in which to serve the ice cream.

After numerous experiments with biscuits, waffles shaped like a cup, he ended up with the waffle or wafer cone idea (that we see today) because it was more practical to eat from that and consume it as well.

Or the story of the sandwich, which was named after the Earl of Sandwich, who inadvertently invented sandwiches when he asked for a piece of meat between slices of bread so that he could continue his game instead of stopping for lunch.

To come up with a story about your product or service, start with the problems it solves or the needs it fulfills to come up with a story.

Borrow from the customer

Your customers can also be the best source of inspiration for your marketing story. These are one of the best marketing weapons you can have in your arsenal as they talk about the success of your customer who used your product or service.

One of the best-loved story categories among marketing folks is about the ways in which they solved a customer's problem, either directly or indirectly.

To come up with customer stories, you will need to talk frequently with customer service and sales folks as they may have the best stories to offer. The story of how inventory software helped an employee in a candy story close up the store earlier so that her son does not need to sit around getting bored is a good example.

When it comes to customer stories, do make sure that you have the explicit permission of the story for marketing purposes before you use it.

The shop floor has a lot to offer

One of the most amazing stories that came out of Amazon is how the founder Jeff Bezos insists on taking customer calls on a regular basis so that he knows the pulse of the market. According to the story, he approached one of the customer associates and asked him to relinquish his phone and computer so that he could take calls.

As Jeff's conversation with the customer progressed, the customer service associate realized that the customer was talking about a particular product that had problems regularly. He commented on it and went on to advise Jeff on how to solve it.

Once the call was completed, Jeff asked the associate about his comment, and based on the history of problems with this product, he established a protocol, which would allow the associate to pull an Andon cord. Pulling an Andon card (a production line term) would mean that the product would not be offered for sale till further investigations were carried out.

You can check with your shopfloor and come up with exciting stories that would add flavor and character to your company, not to mention, bolster your marketing efforts.

Add some twists to make the truth more interesting

There are some readymade stories that you may find within your company, customers, promoters, or the shop floor. But in most instances, the stories though sincere and genuine, may lack the punch you require for your marketing purposes.

When you are in the process of collecting the stories, you can add some flavor and twists to them to make them more attractive. It is the role of marketing in any company to take something and present it in the most beautiful way possible. And augmenting your marketing stories definitely comes under this category.

A story comes into its own only when it has some twists and turns to offer (the struggle is essential) before ending on a happy note. Make sure that you keep it within the realm of reality to make it more acceptable. It is a delicate balance, but that is all part of your marketing efforts.

The journey also counts

Sometimes it is the incredible journey that your company has gone through that makes the story so compelling. Take, for instance, the story of Oprah Winfrey. The incredible and often heartbreaking journey she has gone through is what makes her story so compelling.

You cannot help feeling admiration, sympathy, anger, and respect as you read about the horrors she has faced and the position she has achieved. Your company's journey may not be this eventful, but nevertheless, it is worth portraying as part of your marketing efforts.

The story can be as simple as a group of nerds using IoT to determine if the drink in the refrigerator was cold enough before realizing the potential of the technology, or it can be the way somebody started making herbal cosmetics due to sensitive skin. Both stories have an interesting twist, with one discovering something awesome playfully and the other realizing that others may have the same unique makeup needs they had themselves.

Conclusion

As you dive deeper into the realm of marketing stories, I am sure that you will find many examples that will inspire and delight you. Some companies have made the human angle of their company a compelling marketing story and leveraged it to add a social perspective to their marketing efforts.

The one thing you have to remember about stories in marketing is that nobody will like them or believe them unless you do. So, when you are putting together your story, talk to your team, discuss it with them, find out if they are engaged and emotionally involved before you work on visual and content creatives.

Only when everyone is passionately engaged in the process would it become possible to make the story a marketing weapon.

Test your knowledge with this simple test

34. What makes marketing both love and war?

    a. Marketing is love because you have to love lying and it is war because the market likes it when you come across as aggressive and adventurous

    b. Marketing is love because there are many beautiful objects like models, and visually attractive collateral that you create and the competitiveness makes it a war

    c. Marketing is equated with war because of the fierce competition you face and the adverse conditions you overcome to make an impact. It is compared to love because marketing requires passion and dedication to succeed

    d. Marketing is equated with love and war because there is a huge mixture of positive and negative emotions involved in it

35. What type of marketing stories can you share?

    a. You need to concentrate on the product-related information so that the story has relevance

    b. It is all about the significant achievements and milestones of your company throughout its history from the time of inception to date

   c. You can talk about customers or the process that you followed or stories about the promoter or borrow incidents from the shopfloor

   d. All the above

36. How can you incorporate product development stories in your marketing campaign?

   a. You can include the process and history of product development or the problem you solved or the customer success stories that carry the most weight

   b. You can talk about the complete technology and add the components to it to add meat to the story

   c. You can compare your product with that of the competitor and then put their product down while praising yours

   d. You can forget about product and only talk about the celebrities that used your company's product or services

Don't Forget the Numbers When it Comes to Results

"What use is a pretty garden if it does not yield fruits and flowers to eat and enjoy?"

What is marketing? Is it an art, or is it science? This is a question that has haunted many people over the ages., but ask a marketer, he or she will tell you it is both. That, according to marketers, is the most attractive aspect of marketing.

They love the whimsy and the quirks of being artists who take the mundane (in many instances) and present it in the best possible light to their audience on the one hand. On the other, they are the saviors of the holy grail of most businesses—the bottom-line—because they are responsible for selling their products or services.

Don't forget the numbers when it comes to results

While marketing is an art that you need to carry out with creativity, it is nothing without the numbers. Keep a watch on your numbers, keep changing your approach to up the numbers, and share your numbers on all public forums.

I have said this before, and I will say it again, marketing is not for the faint-hearted because it literally needs you to sail in two boats. That is why I am going to dedicate this chapter to the numbers that marketing folks have to focus on.

Take your attention away from those, and all your efforts are going to be for naught. The genius lies in being on helm of the ship with all the details, from the creatives to the numbers.

Here's what, we as marketers need to focus on in terms of numbers:

Start with what you spend

For a marketer, creating and maintaining a budget may not always be the most pleasant of activities, but it is the most important. Why is it so critical? It is essential because marketing is about kindling a need in people and turning it into want and then ensuring that they buy.

Without measuring what you spent and what you earned, you will not be able to evaluate how effective all your efforts were. That is the logical explanation, but there is another aspect, which is the emotional side of it.

As I stated earlier, marketers are artists at some level, and would definitely want to know how well-like their art is. Now that I have clarified why tracking what you spend is essential, let us look at what you need to monitor:

Team

Many marketers ignore the cost of people working in the marketing department because they feel that they are only opting for organic ways to market their brand, products, or services. While it is true that organic methods of marketing require no cost in terms of advertisement, it does require the efforts of your team.

Your team, in most instances, would consist of the content and copywriters, graphic designers, video experts, automation experts, and the campaign team. The campaign team could be further divided into your paid campaign experts and organic marketing people. It goes without saying that in many smaller marketing organizations, many people play multiple roles.

For instance, your copywriters could take care of ad copy, content, and even design. Or the same person could manage your web management and public relations and so on.

The question here is whether you want to have an in-house team who does all these activities, or you want to outsource some to an agency. Having an in-house team would mean fixed expenses on the one hand, but you are also assured of the quality and timeliness of the work.

Having an agency to provide services could help cut down expenses but would also mean compromising on quality and delays in the delivery of marketing collateral when you need them at once.

There is a third option available where you can have a mix of an in-house team along with an agency for some part of your marketing work. Consider all the expenses including bonuses, retainer amounts, and overtime payments

Tools

Today, digital marketing depends on many tools and sites to help create and use quality campaign materials. For instance, you have stock photos, stock video clips, copy check software, etc. You do need the right quality tools to enhance the creative efforts of your team, whether it is managing the website or creating videos.

However, if you are sharing the tools with some other departments, do consider apportioning part of the expenses to them based on the usage. Again, you can minimize the fixed costs on many tools by only opting for free or trial versions.

Alternatively, you can consider subscribing to them for a shorter period and getting all your related work at that time. No matter which path you take, ensure that you evaluate the tools you are using for quality, reliability, and price before you make any decisions.

Advertisements

Advertisements are probably one of the most significant costs that marketing incurs, along with the team costs. However, paid ads online, offline, and on social media are among the most effective ways to quickly reach your intended audience.

Track what costs you are incurring for ads, including the cost of creatives to add to your marketing budget. Make sure that you are completely thorough when you look at the expense of advertisements online as well as offline.

Many companies find that hoardings, standees, and other physical methods of displaying their brand, helps them build immense brand recognition. While you could also consider adding this expense under the corporate image building section, some part of the cost will become part of the marketing budget, especially when the marketing department also owns complete responsibility for brand building.

Agency

Even if your model of working uses only in-house employees for all marketing-related activities, there is a chance that you may still incur some agency-related costs. For instance, you could use an agency to purchase hoarding positions in a particular area.

Or you could depend on a modeling agency to provide models for photoshoots and advertisements. In some companies, the concept of web-hosting agency is adopted due to a lack of expertise in this area, and this could be an agency cost that you will have to consider.

Offline costs

This portion could include events that the marketing department has participated in or hosted. It can be a considerable part of your budget, depending on the kind of events you have in your industry and how beneficial they are to your business.

Event costs could include the price of all the materials you create, accommodations, the fee that you pay to the event organizers, and so on.

Look again, you may have missed something

I added this section because many costs become part of marketing that we regularly forget to include. Take, for instance, the cost of traveling. Or the money you spend on sponsorship.

Or the cost of branded merchandise that we use as giveaways to create brand awareness. Or the fees we pay to consultants or the cost of printing.

Then look at what leads your efforts brought in

Now that we have looked at what we spent, it is time to do the fun bit—the leads our efforts bring in. Marketing departments look at numerous factors when it comes to the impact they have created.

For instance, when it comes to the website, they look at the number of visits, the time spent on the page, the pages the visitor moved on to, and the next steps (clicks) the visitor took to go further in his journey among other factors.

Another number that becomes important is the way you rank in Google search results—the higher you show up and in the top pages, the better. In the same way, interactions and views on social media is also another number that we, as marketers, track.

But the number that is closest to our hearts is the MQLs or marketing qualified leads. These are the leads that have taken the next steps and qualify to be called viable leads.

Trace them to ensure the completion

Does the role of marketing end with the hand over of qualified leads to the sales team? Actually, we still need to keep an eye on the next steps. We want to ensure that we provide the sales team enough support to make these leads into sales-qualified and then on to actual sales.

Drill down to revenues generated

By now, you guessed the next step—track the revenue that your successful leads have generated! You may wonder why you need to do this? Well, the next time, there is a question of what value the marketing department adds, then you can talk about the revenues generated and the return on investment.

Add in the intangibles for good measure

Don't just stop with the revenues because marketing is not just about the generation of revenues. It is about brand reach and awareness. Do keep measuring and recording results. Look at the way people talk about your brand and products.

Keep an eye out on forums and associations where people are likely to talk about your brand.

Present the ROI of marketing efforts

Now that you have an idea of what was spent and how much business marketing efforts have helped bring in, you need to market your department. Ensure that you present a realistic but attractive picture of marketing efforts. It always comes in handy when you are discussing next year's budgets.

In conclusion, I would go so far as to say that marketing is nothing without the numbers to back it up. If anything, marketing starts with numbers (audience size, areas, products, services, budgets, limits, etc.) and ends with numbers (expenditure, leads, revenue, brand value, etc.).

If you are planning a career in marketing, you need to equip yourself to be comfortable around numbers. You need to be able to dig deeper and come up with the best ways to put forth what you and your team have achieved. No digital marketing education would be complete without a hefty dose of analytics. Luckily wrapping your head around numbers is a skill that you can learn with ease.

What is more, the market offers many paid and free tools that will let you keep track of numbers.

Here are some simple steps that you can take to ensure that you and your entire team is familiar with numbers:

- Create a shared budget sheet with expenses (you may have to remove salary details from there)
- Encourage all the members in your team to look at analytics regularly
- Push the team to come up with conclusions, inferences, and call-outs from these numbers
- Teach them to talk numbers with ease and help them to figure out how to back it up with the right explanation
- If budget allows, get the right tools for them to collect and interpret data in the right way
- Make it mandatory for all the members in your team (content, design, automation, web management, public relations, etc.) to present numbers regularly

Test Boldly and Test Often to See What Works

14

"To commit mistakes is progress, but to not learn from them and move ahead will cause regrets."

If you meet a marketer (or a person) who says they have never made mistakes, then they are liars or lazy people. In fact, they are liars because nobody can be that lazy and still be part of marketing. Does this mean that you should make mistakes in your marketing approach?

No, it does not mean that you should make mistakes, but that mistakes will happen. When a mistake does happen, you need to carefully take a step back and examine what went wrong. You need to pinpoint the exact person or event that caused it (not to place blame) and analyze what could have been done so that you can learn from it.

In marketing, there will be many instances where you will feel that you are stepping into uncharted territories. It could be anything—a new product, a new approach, a new area, or a new industry—but the idea is that you need to test the waters to see what works and what does not.

"

Test boldly and test often to see what works

There is no single marketing formula that will lead to instant success. The best way to ensure that you are getting it right is to keep testing new approaches with smaller audiences.

"
It's through m*stakes that you actually can grow.

Let me give you an example that I heard years ago (in the early 90s) about how GE finance in India, had a tough time entering the personal finance market at the beginning. Their approach was basic. They had a simple form that potential customers had to fill, which asked for personal and professional details.

Using the information on the form and a few other checks and details, the credit manager would decide if the person qualified for a loan or not. To the surprise of the head office, there seemed to be no takers to the loans. They decided to check with the local office to see whether their interest rates and other terms of the loan were not attractive.

To their consternation, the GE finance head office discovered that the interest rates and terms of the loan were better than many of their local competitors in India. After much head-scratching, the GE guys decided to ask the customers directly. The inputs they got left them stunned.

Most people refused to avail of the personal loan because of the form that GE finance asked them to fill. The questionnaire asked for their marital status, with options including single, married, divorced; it went on to dig deeper to ask them about alimony payments in case a person was divorced.

To the minds of a very conservative society that India was at that time, asking someone if they were divorced was a bad omen, especially when they are planning to do something as auspicious as buying a vehicle or improving their homes. Since GE finance was asking them to fill the form with all the details, they had decided that they would refuse the loan rather than answer such impudent and inauspicious questions.

From the GE Finance point of view, the alimony information was critical for them to determine if the borrower could pay back the loan after all commitments were met. After a few discussions with the local office, they decided that they would create a new form without the marital status column to see how it worked.

It would be a pilot project, which would keep track to see if the bad debts went up or not before fully launching it. Three months into the test, the head office was stunned at the number of loans they had disbursed, and in another three months, they could see that repayment was not a problem at all. The conclusion?

The head office guys decided it is better to test the local market to see what works and what doesn't instead of assuming that one size fits all.

The lesson I am going for here is that it is a good idea to keep coming up with new ideas and testing them time and again to see if it works or not. And don't just restrict your testing to tweaks you have made only to launches and projects that are not working but also to those that work.

In case one of your campaigns is a roaring success, then don't take it off the market but launch another with a few tweaks to see if it works. You will be pleasantly surprised at the number of positive changes you are able to make once you start testing boldly.

Let us dive a little deeper into the many ways you can test your marketing ideas and initiatives. Here are some ways I can think of, and I am sure that as you evolve as a marketing leader, you will have many more ideas to add to this.

Try a new tone of voice

Do you believe that brands have personalities? I definitely think they do. And it is the responsibility of the marketer to establish a positive and distinctive personality and tone of voice for the brand. Brands try to build their persona and tone of voice in all their marketing materials.

For instance, the recent campaign by Burger King established them as bold and even stark. While the ad had us retching and cringing, it did make a statement—a very bold one—considering it is part of the food industry.

"It's not what you say, It's how you say it."

It does not matter if the product or service you are marketing is B2C or B2B, the customer profile keeps on changing. What is seen as unacceptable today may become popular tomorrow. And if you are a bit hesitant about changing your tone of voice, start small.

One of the simplest ways to do it is by posting a blog on your company website as a guest blog (that way, you may not shock people too much) and share it on social media as well to see what the reactions are. Or you could come up with a really bold concept video that you show at a particular event where the audience is limited.

This will give you a way out if you find that the reaction is negative, to discontinue the strategy. And if testing on a live audience is a step too far for your company and industry, you can always go for test groups. The only problem with this is that the reaction that you get may not cover a broader cross-section of people.

Nevertheless, you can overcome this limitation by being careful in the selection of people in your test group.

Tweak your imagery

How you portray your brand in pictures is a big part of how your audience perceives you, and this is another area that you can test all the time. You can start small and go with a different kind of image than the one you usually use.

Brands often work with a particular set of colors, and you could experiment with this aspect if you are feeling bold. Videos also tend to follow a pattern for brands, with some, going for a matter of fact tone and others going for quirky.

These media also offer you plenty of chances to test the marketing idea out and see how they react. We know of brands that went from businesslike to humane in a video only to get outstanding reactions to this.

Of course, if your intention is to change the whole brand, including the logo of the brand, then you can build up the changes in the brand image through a series of communications, posts, and paid ads before going for the finale.

Experiment with new channels

Tired of posting only on Facebook or LinkedIn? Then go for more picture-oriented sites like Pinterest or Instagram. Instead of blogging just on your company blog, go ahead and share something on another blog, with permissions, of course, to see what happens.

Start answering questions on Quora or do a complete turnaround and move away to Twitter for some time. If you want, you can post the same content at the same time on all the channels to see how each works. This way, you know which channels best suit which content. The results may pleasantly surprise you or leave you reeling with shock.

As I said in the earlier chapter, analytics are essential, and you need to continually look at them to see what works. You have to be prepared for some of your tests and experiments to fail. Put it down as experience and a lesson and move on to the next one.

Keep checking the internet to see the next new channel you can experiment with and do give it a try. The only limitations for your testing should be harmful results or a complete lack of resources and not a dearth of ideas.

Come up with different promotions

Promotional offers are the seasoning for most B2C products because it makes it that much more palatable to consume. We wait for the next promotional offer before making our move to purchase the product. The use of promotions in the B2B market is not so prevalent. However, you could always try it out to see how it works.

For example, you could offer an extra week of usage along with the purchase of three months' license to use your software. In crisis situations, companies may just lap up even the smallest offers, and this could become a deal breaker for you.

I need not tell you much the value of testing with various promotions in the B2C market.

Build up your portfolio

Another way to test your marketing ideas is to add to your portfolio, though strictly speaking, it is not a completely marketing-related idea. But as part of the marketing, you would be in the right position to get inputs from customers about what they expect.

You could always present these ideas to the right people in the company, and help them market the additions or changes to your existing product mix. This is a good way for you to do some test marketing and ensure that your company does not become stagnant and keeps up with the changing market trends.

Change those forms

If you are following the inbound method of marketing, then leading the customer through his or her buyer's journey is part of your marketing activities. One of the ways the customer expresses interest in getting further information is by filling a form with contact information to get marketing collateral in return. In most instances, the collateral will help the customer make an informed decision on the purchase that he or she is contemplating.

Instead of a regular run-of-the-mill form, you can make it a little quirkier and more personal to test how it works out. Sometimes, doing this will perk the customer's interest and drive them to fill the form.

You can even experiment with the messaging once the form is filled to make it more engaging and informative.

Add humor to see how it works

The general belief of people other than marketing folks is that marketing is all about fun and creativity. While this is not entirely wrong, it is not the complete truth either. The fact is marketing is a serious business that can involve a lot of creativity, and depending on the product, some fun.

However, even if you are part of the oh-so-serious B2B marketing segment, you can cautiously test the market with bits of humor to engage your potential customer and see how it works. I have deliberately used the word 'cautiously' here because you need to be very careful when experimenting with humor.

What is one culture's joke is another culture's slur. One famous example that comes to mind is that of a soft drink's advertisement in the desert-ridden areas. Apparently, they had a series of pictures depicting a person roaming the desert, feeling thirsty, falling down, then coming across the soft drink, having it, and feeling refreshed.

But in some cultures and languages, the norm is to read in reverse, which means that customers saw a person drinking the soft drink, feeling parched, and then getting lost in the hot sands. The result—no sales. A word to the wise is to test humorous captions, and depictions with people you know personally before even consider test marketing it.

Be different to see if it pays off

The noise, as I said earlier, is too much in the market, and we need to be heard. But even that, you need to approach with caution. You can use marketing to portray your brand as different from the rest of the direct competitors. However, this may not always be seen as an asset.

Which is why I am asking you to test the waters before jumping in completely.

15 Last But Not Least, Spend Well and Wisely

"Money need not be the root of all evil if you learn to use it well and don't let it use you."

Can you market a product or service well, without spending on it? If you are answering in the affirmative, then either your ambitions to market your product are very limited, or you are ignorant. Yes, you can work with a minimal budget, but you cannot carry on marketing activities without spending.

In this chapter, I will be ending with the last commandment of growth marketing, which is about spending well and wisely. I know that it is easier said than done, but as marketers, the onus is on us to keep a delicate balance between being practical and creative without letting anything slip.

Last but not least, spend well and wisely

Nothing worth doing well can be done for free. There is a definite cost to marketing, but what you can do is that you plan your budgets well and spend wisely.

However, before we plunge into the world of managing budgets and balancing the outcomes against limited resources, let us take a look at some of the nifty marketing examples where the brand has managed to make an impact with minimal spending.

I am sure there are many brands that are doing that, but the two examples that come to mind are Krispy Kreme and Costco. These two brands are doing really well but do not have considerable spending on advertising. How do they do that?

You must be thinking that they offer value, which is why they don't need to have a huge marketing budget. If you examine these two examples, you will realize that they do have a marketing strategy in place, but it is not the traditional one, and it does not involve that much spending.

Let us first start with Krispy Kreme. First and foremost, they have nailed the product—you cannot say the name without drooling—and the product stands by the promise of the name. And then there is the way they have trained each of their staff to attend to customer needs in the best possible way.

The third aspect that they have invested in is the location. By doing this, you are naturally providing easy access to something that we all want. Then there is the way they have showcased their product creation process to the customer. In this case, they have fully leveraged the maxim that you eat with your eyes first. Then comes the final bit, which is word of mouth.

Costco, on the other hand, went for the membership model combined with hard-to-resist prices, good stock, and creating an easy shopping experience. The idea of a store like this requiring membership appeals to the FOMO (fear of missing out) factor to most people.

Add to that the fact that they have a captive audience, who have memberships, to whom they can send offers and promotional material. It is a stroke of genius, and it has worked very well for them.

Now that I have given you some examples, here are some tips that you can use to spend well and wisely. I have already scattered some advice on this throughout the book, like the ones about having your employees going social, the big gestures, the storytelling, to name a few.

However, in this chapter, I will nudge you towards looking at your business specifically and then planning on the way you are going to spend your marketing budget to get the best returns.

Start with the customer and work backward

As people, we are creatures of habit, and even the most adventurous among us want that hint of familiarity. We like to know that some things will only occur in some places.

And when this happens, there is a certain feeling of safety and security. For instance, the mediocre coffee we get on flights. We expect and accept it.

Where I am going with all this is that customers as a group are used to certain behavior and approaches. As a marketer, you need to get into the mindset of the customer.

Let me give you a negative example here: You are hardly likely to make a success of your fitness equipment shop near a video game arcade, but on the other hand, having it right outside a food court may not be such a bad idea.

We all love junk food, but for most of us, the consumption of junk food is followed by a bout of guilt, and this is followed by a resolution to do more physical activity. Voila! A stop at the fitness shop to buy fitness equipment right in the vicinity is an excellent way to assuage your guilt.

This was a very simplistic and basic example, but it is just to show you how much you need to get into the customer mindset. For example, if you are selling surgical equipment, you will not find much traffic in a mall.

One of the proven ways to examine what customers think and understanding their minds is to do a survey. But if you do not have the means to do this, you can simply gather a set of people at different levels, and you can go through the purchase process with a competitor. Make sure that you do not let your personal prejudices creep in, but think like your customer would.

Don't be entirely led by the competition

Even as I am advising you to look at the competition to understand what the customer thinks like, I must caution you that you should not be entirely led by the competition. Why is this important? There are several reasons for this. First of all, you do not want your brand to be seen as a me-too.

Secondly, your brand and your closest competitor will have fundamental differences not only in terms of how old the company is but also in terms of the budgets they have, the kind of management they have, the type of marketing team they have, and much more.

Guidance from the competition or a starting point for your thinking can be right but not copying entirely. When you do that, there is no differentiating factor for the customer, and this may lead to poor market perception, especially if you are not able to provide the same experience to your customer.

If you look at similar situations in the past, this has often led to pricing wars, with all the parties concerned making considerable losses in a bid to upstage each other.

Make sure your basics are sound and sustainable

When we are talking about marketing spend and budgets, we are talking about all how you will promote the products or services that your company offers.

However, there are some basics like the quality of your products or services, your customer service, your policies for after-sales support, and more.

Even as you market your product, you need to ensure that your company is in a position to deliver on the promises you make. This needs to be sound and sustainable to work in the long-term. I know that strictly speaking, this part does not fall under marketing responsibilities, but being aware of these factors will help you tone down your messaging.

What is more, in the case of mishaps, marketing will be prepared with messaging and strategies for damage control.

Be flexible and creative in your approach

The market, as we know, and therefore, customers are always changing. For instance, the crisis the world is facing today has changed the way customers buy things. In some cases, we have seen an excess of purchasing and the inability of the market to meet the burgeoning demands, and on the other hand, we have seen a complete stoppage of buying decisions.

As a marketer, flexible and creative have to be the keywords you live by. Without these two qualities, you will find that managing your budgets and the way you spend will become very difficult. In certain situations, you may have to assume various roles and perform tasks that are not routine for you to ensure that you curb expenditure.

Revisit several times if required

No marketing plan or budget is set in stone. While there could be an upper and lower limit fixed, it would be wise to review your plans frequently. In the ordinary course of events, this will mean nothing more than tracking the returns you are getting on ad spend and monitoring what changes to make, but it is essential.

Just visualize this. You have created a series of paid ads based on a set of keywords that you believe (based on research) that will work for your company. But once you have launched the campaign, you realize that there are too many unrelated clicks, and the ads are not effective. The best step here would be to stop the ads until such time that you can dig deeper.

Or imagine a situation where your organic traffic is bringing more leads than paid ads. Then, in this case, your frequent assessments will show you that you can stop the costly ads and use the funds to create relevant content for sharing organically.

A wise marketer will revisit his or her plans and budgets at regular intervals to ensure that he or she is spending well and wisely.

Borrow, mix, and match to make your plan

Don't know where to start? That's okay too. Today, the internet provides us with a wealth of information (sometimes, too much), which means that you can borrow ideas from others. Just because you adopt one of the factors from one of your competitors does not mean that you have duplicate everything.

For instance, you could borrow an organic campaign approach from a similar industry, but your paid ad campaign can be based on your immediate competition, and your social media campaign could be from elsewhere entirely.

When you are doing this, ensure that you have your team providing inputs and insights so that there is acceptance as well as structure to your plan.

Conclusion

As the book comes to a conclusion, I wish to reiterate what I said in the beginning. While I encourage you to read the entire book, adopt those parts that fit into your overall strategy and the needs of your business.

Answers to the exercise questions

Chapter 1

Question 1: Why do you need to be loud as a marketer in today's world? Because:

Answer: b. The market is crowded

Question 2: Why does being truthful and vulnerable matter? Because:

Answer: d. Truth can make you look sincere and being vulnerable adds a human element

Question 3: How do you balance your loud brand personality to make it more likable?

Answer: c. Add a personal touch to make your brand approachable

Chapter 2

Question 4: What are the two segments of the market that you can copy from?

Answer: c. Companies that are in direct competition with you and companies that are doing well in a similar niche.

Question 5: Which one of these represents competitors and companies for a similar niche?

Answer: b. Suzlon-Whole Foods and Samsung-Apple

Question 6: What steps should you follow to come up with the right marketing strategy?

Answer: a. Observe, curate, discuss, test, add some value, and launch

Chapter 3

Question 7: Why do you need to hope for the best but plan for the worst?

Answer: c. It is always better to have a back-up plan when things don't go as planned

Question 8: What should the ideal marketing team consist of?

Answer: c. A mix of various skillsets and personalities to help maintain the balance

Question 9: How to get started with the right customer experience?

Answer: b. Research, test marketing, insights from competitors, and trials will help you

Chapter 4:

Question 10: Who in your team needs to be seen and heard on social media?

Answer: c. Most of your team if not the entire team, needs to be smartly present on social media

Question 11: What are the rules to follow for your team participating in controversial topics on social media?

Answer: b. Be careful in the way you address controversies. If possible, seek the help of your content team to come up with quirky and witty answers that are not offensive

Question 12: What should a company's policy be on press releases?

Answer: a. Share within the company internally and externally at the same time and then brief people to share on social media

Chapter 5

Question 13: When does the customer's purchase journey start?

Answer: d. All of the above

Question 14: How can you help customers make the right purchase decision?

Answer: c. Become the authority on the product and offer them the various choices that he or she has and be honest about the features of your product

Question 15: What aspects of cost and features should you discuss?

Answer: c. Be honest about your intentions and talk about the amount your customer will have to spend and what he or she will get in return

Chapter 6

Question 16: What techniques do you need to use to add a tag of exclusivity to your product or service?

Answer: a. Show the efforts that have gone into creating it, and the various steps involved, price it right and showcase the value

Question 17: What role can the story of your product development play in marketing?

Answer: b. It can build value and human interest in the way your product was built and help attract leads

Question 18: How important is it for your marketing team to believe in the concept they are selling?

Answer: b. It is integral to the success of your marketing efforts as it lends your campaign with a solid base

Chapter 7

Question 19: What factors should you keep in mind while going for those extras?

Answer: b. Plan according to the product, culture, occasion, and use your discretion to do this

Question 20: Why do you need to share customer success stories online?

Answer: c. To ensure that you keep building on credibility and goodwill for your brand

Question 21: Why do the little extras and special treatments matter a lot in marketing?

Answer: a. It shows that you care and displays the depth of understanding you have about the customer's needs.

Chapter 8

Question 22: How do you build a brand identity, starting with what you do?

Answer: a. Start with the specifics, define what it does, broaden the scope, and aspirational value

Question 23: What is the correlation between brand identity and customer persona?

Answer: b. It is similar to the connection to the body type you and the clothing that will work for it

Question 24: How do you ensure that everyone in your company has an idea of brand personality?

Answer: d. Discuss, debate, and formalize this so that you can share it as part of the onboarding process

Chapter 9

Question 25: What does celebrity persona have to do with marketing?

Answer: a. It touches upon aspirations people have, and by using a celebrity for publicity, you can relate the product with the aspirations of the buyer

Question 26: What is the key to making the celebrity endorsement work for your brand?

Answer: c. Match the product with the personality to ensure that it touches an emotional chord in the customer's minds

Question 27: What is the option if you cannot afford to have a celebrity as part of your marketing campaigns?

Answer: b. Create your own version of a relatable celebrity with smart storytelling and a persona

Chapter 10

Question 28: What are the factors to consider when you segment your market as per your product?

Answer: a. Ability to pay, willingness to buy, and access to the next-level consumers along with an understanding of the product potential and the right vision

Question 29: Why is identifying the right niche critical?

Answer: b. It brings focus to marketing, gets better ROI, meets the right customers' needs, and helps build a better brand image

Question 30: What impact does getting the niche right have on your marketing budgets?

Answer: c. Getting the niche right will ensure that your marketing campaigns are more focused and you have a better reach.

Chapter 11

Question 31: What kind of personality does a marketer need to have?

Answer: b. Confident, focused, well-organized, numbers-oriented, and strategic in their approach to each task

Question 32: You should never allow your team to talk about the efforts in the creation of marketing assets? Right?

Answer: b. Wrong! You want your team to feel good about themselves and showcase the process they followed to create marketing materials while harnessing the power of their contacts and social reach once you have launched the campaign

Question 33: What should you and your team do once they have shared marketing-related posts on personal social media accounts?

Answer: b. They should encourage conversations, engage, and answer to comments with a calm and composed manner while sharing the right information

Chapter 12

Question 34: What makes marketing both love and war?

Answer: c. Marketing is equated with war because of the fierce competition you face and the adverse conditions you overcome to make an impact. It is compared to love because marketing requires passion and dedication to succeed

Question 35: What type of marketing stories can you share?

Answer: d. All the above

Question 36: How can you incorporate product development stories in your marketing campaign?

Answer: a. You can include the process and history of product development or the problem you solved or the customer success stories that carry the most weight